Oregon City

Oldest known photograph of Oregon City. It was made in 1857 by Lorenzo Lorain.

Oregon City

(By Way of the Barlow Road)
At The End of the National Historic

Oregon Trail

Bert and Margie Webber

Webb Research Group
Publishers of Books About the
Oregon Country

Please address all inquiries to the publisher:
WEBB RESEARCH GROUP
P. O. Box 314
Medford, ORegon 97501 U.S.A.

Library of Congress Cataloging in Publication Data:

Webber, Bert.
    Oregon Trail (by way of the Barlow Road), at the end of the National
Historic Oregon Trail / Bert and Margie Webber.
    p.   cm.
    Includes bibliographical references (p.   ) and index.
    ISBN: 0-936738-71-5
    1. Oregon City (Or.)—History. 2. Oregon Trail. [3. Barlow Road]. I.
Webber, Margie. II. Title.
F884.06W33 1993   92-33561
979.5'41—dc20   CIP—Rev.
_____ [Published in 1993] _____

Contents

The J. H. Richardson drawing of Oregon City in 1845.

Sir. Henry Warre sketch of Oregon City in 1846.
Original hangs in Library of Congress

Introduction

Oregon City is an intriguing town for, among many reasons, it has a municipal elevator that jumps people from the ground level of the city 100 feet straight up to the next level. San Francisco may have a crooked street but Oregon City has its elevator. And, come to think of it, both San Francisco and Oregon City had private operating mints as early as 1849. Another uniqueness is that when the town of Yerba Buena, the earlier name for San Francisco, was laid out, the plat was sent to Oregon City to be recorded as Oregon City had the first land office in the west. Oregon City's beginning could be called an intrigue that was played out between Dr. John McLoughlin, the Chief Factor ("President") of the Columbia Department of the Hudson's Bay Company of London, England and a Methodist missionary, the Rev. Alvin F. Waller. (Waller worked for Jason Lee of the Methodist Mission that had been established upriver from Oregon City in 1834.) There is little doubt that McLoughlin was there first – 1829 – and allowed Waller, a squatter, who did not arrive until 1840, to use some of McLoughlin's pre-cut logs to put up a building. But by "making right the master of might," which included the authority of a newly formed provisional government, the Americans shoved McLoughlin out even though McLoughlin had alread laid out the town and people were living in it.

McLoughlin was not about to quit. With his circumstances at Fort Vancouver changing, he adopted a "turn the other cheek" attitude and retired from his Hudson's Bay Company post – under pressure for having helped the Americans contrary to what the Honourable Company believed were its best interests – and settled down on his claim in Oregon City. Until the organization of the provisional government, Dr. John McLoughlin was loosely considered by most people as Oregon's first governor for he had ruled all of the Oregon Country from his desk at Fort Vancouver. Today he is recalled as Oregon City's first citizen and is remembered throughout the state by streets and schools named for him as well as Mount McLoughlin (9,495 feet elev.) in Jackson County.

Rev. Mr. Waller had been assigned to set up a mission station at the falls of the Willamette for the purpose of working with the Indians. Yarnes points out:

> The Methodist work in the area was mostly on the west side of the river [and] Waller's claim at Willamette Falls had no connection with the Methodist Mission as such.

It has been suggested that Waller wanted to control the massive water power of the falls. Yarnes wrote:

> [Jason] Lee believed that the claim of a British citizen (McLoughlin) would be regarded as invalid after the boundary question was settled if his claim was contested.... Lee himself did not file on the coveted area for the Methodist Mission [and] he had no idea when he appointed Waller to [head the] Willamette Falls Mission that this man of initiative would file a claim to the property.

But care needs to be exercised not to be judgmental, at this late date, as to Waller's activities which were extensive and as he and Jason Lee believed, were intended to further the interests of the mission. As we shall see in the text, he was superintendent at The Dalles Mission when Joel Palmer and Sam Barlow appeared on the scene in 1845. Among other activities, Waller was on the Board of Trustees when Willamette University was granted its charter in 1853. Nevertheless, as to being remembered in Oregon City today, other than as the founding pastor in 1840 of the Methodist Church there, no streets, mountains, rivers or creeks have been named for him.

In this short work on Oregon City we have tried to include pertinences that will give flavor to this exciting town and to provide references in the bibliography for those who want to pursue the history in greater detail.

We are indebted to a number of people who assisted with pulling together the many miscellaneous items in this book including historical and contemporary photographs.

Wilmer Gardner, Milwaukie, past president of the Clackamas County Historical Society, was a colleague with Bert Webber when they served together on the Board of Directors of the society in the 1960's. He graciously offered selections from his unique picture collection which help make this an effective volume. We appreciate his careful attention to detail and his help.

Robert Monaghan, Director of the Clackamas County Historical Society, offered the use of the detailed map of the Barlow Road for which the society holds the copyright. James Weeks, The Dalles, provided additional help with the Barlow Road chapter and loaned

Main Street Oregon City 1867. Dr. John McLoughlin's house is left of center. Village on left above falls is Canemah.

photographs as did Claire Met of Oregon City. Doug Jones, "Barlow Road Wagonmaster" from Bear Springs Ranger District of Mt. Hood National Forest, provided maps and other valuable assistance. We thank these folks for their respective contributions.

We wish to thank Virginia Broadhouse, Canemah, for her help in identifying the area of this unique section of Oregon City and for loaning photographs of her home, an "original" from the historic ship building period.

John Labbe, Beaverton, railroad historian and oft published author, was immediately willing to provide photographs of several of the electric interurban trains and street cars that served Oregon City.

The rare postmarks and stamps were loaned by Leonard Lukens, Phoenix, Oregon to assist the chapter on the post office. We appreciate the trust of Labbe and Lukens for the loan of these rare photos, postmarks and stamps which provide great flavor to this book.

Nancy Wilson, curator of the McLoughlin Memorial Association, provided details about the life of Dr. John McLoughlin, photographs of the McLoughlin House and loaned copies of some out-of-print books. She served as a valuable consultant on the McLoughlin chapter for which we appreciate her interest and help.

We appreciate the long-standing friendship of Richard J. Portal, Salem, master reference librarian (retired). He made inquiries in that city for early Oregon City material, especially for copies of Oregon's first newspaper, the *Oregon Spectator.*

We want to thank Roger McClurg, Library Director at Oregon City Public Library, who provided some photographs and data about the distinguished history of the library.

We particularly want to remember the various members of the staff of the Reference Department at Jackson County Library System in Medford. These professionals engaged in a diligent pursuit for obscure data that fit this project.

The authors are always open to constructive comments and will accept correspondence sent in care of the publisher. The address is on page iv.

Bert and Margie Webber
Central Point, Oregon
Spring 1993

The Oregon Trail

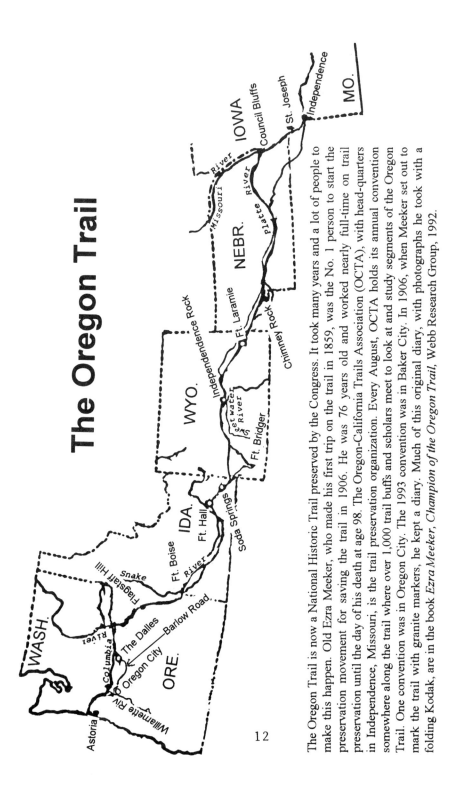

The Oregon Trail is now a National Historic Trail preserved by the Congress. It took many years and a lot of people to make this happen. Old Ezra Meeker, who made his first trip on the trail in 1906, was the No. 1 person to start the preservation movement for saving the trail in 1859. He was 76 years old and worked nearly full-time on trail preservation until the day of his death at age 98. The Oregon-California Trails Association (OCTA), with head-quarters in Independence, Missouri, is the trail preservation organization. Every August, OCTA holds its annual convention somewhere along the trail where over 1,000 trail buffs and scholars meet to look at and study segments of the Oregon Trail. One convention was in Oregon City. The 1993 convention was in Baker City. In 1906, when Meeker set out to mark the trail with granite markers, he kept a diary. Much of this original diary, with photographs he took with a folding Kodak, are in the book *Ezra Meeker, Champion of the Oregon Trail*, Webb Research Group, 1992.

Chapter 1
Exploring for the Barlow Road

Several writers assert that the Oregon Trail ended at The Dalles on the Columbia River. Their reasoning is that in the early days, the only way to the Willamette Valley from that point was by way of the Columbia and Willamette Rivers and required the use of boat as there was no more trail.

Livestock, that had trudged with the people over the plains, wouldn't usually fit in the little boats that were available but could be walked along the bank of the river. Or, could be led over the old Lee Cattle Trail that crossed the Cascade Mountains eventually arriving in the Willamette Valley at Oregon City. But the mountain trail was not suitable for wagons.

The river route was expensive, boats were scarce and when folks had to wait for weeks for a boat, their living expenses at The Dalles could be staggering. Of course the mission took in some, but its facilities were limited.

Those men who had any pioneering spirit left in them after their 2,000 mile 6-months walk, cut pine logs from the forest and built crude rafts or, in some cases, constructed flat-boats made of whipsawed lumber. The wagon could be transported in the boats for a wagon was a necessity for farm work which many of the pioneers would pursue. Nevertheless, a trip down the Columbia River, a roaring torrent in those days, was an hazardous adventure for flat-land people who were definitely not sailors.

The float would proceed as far as the confluence with the Willamette River then the craft had to be rowed and poled against an often swift current up the Willamette River. Their destination was easily found as their craft could go only to the base of Willamette Falls. They were now in the storied Willamette Valley and before them was Oregon City.

Getting over or around Mount Hood seemed a major stumbling block to any who wanted to gain Oregon City by trail and avoid the rivers. Joel Palmer and Samuel Barlow, among many others, were each stuck at The Dalles—no boats and no further trail.

Palmer, a Canadian, was 35 years old when he left his wife in their home in Laurel, Indiana and undertook his first trip to Oregon in early 1845. On that trip he kept a careful diary which he published when he returned to the mid-west in 1846. His guide book carried the title *Journal of Travels Over the Rocky Mountains* and was printed in Cincinnati in 1947. The next year he set out again on the Oregon Trail but this time with his wife and family.

On his 1845 trip, Palmer reached The Dalles but was disappointed in discovering what has been reported to have been as many as sixty families waiting transportation to get on to Oregon City. With winter about to set in, he did not want to delay. He wrote:

Sept. 30: This day we intended to make arrangements for our passage down the river but we found on inquiry that the two boats spoken of were engaged for at least ten days and that their charges were exorbitant, and would probably absorb what little we had left to pay our way to Oregon City. We then determined to make a trip over the mountains and made inquiries respecting its practicability of some Indians but could learn nothing definite, excepting that grass, timber and water would be found in abundance. We finally ascertained that a Mr. Barham [*sic.* Samuel Kimborough Barlow] and Mr. Nighton [Henry Knighton] had, with the same object, penetrated some twenty or twenty-five miles into the interior and found it impracticable. Nighton had returned but Barham was yet in the mountains endeavoring to force a passage. They has been absent for six days with seven wagons in their train intending to go as far as they could and if found to be impracticable to return and go down the river.

Sam Barlow, on arrival at The Dalles, believed there must surely be away though the mountains between Mount Hood and Mount Jefferson. He could not believe that The Dalles was to be considered the end of the Oregon Trail for wagons. His arguments met mixed reaction from those persons he talked to. Many were just, plain, tired out after the 2,000 mile walk from the mid-west. These just wanted to get on to Oregon City without any more trail-trudging especially over an unknown route where there was no road. Nevertheless, of the pack of pioneers at The Dalles at the end of September 1845, there were nineteen people in seven wagons who agreed to go with Sam Barlow. They would be

14

pioneers indeed for this was an exploring expedition to establish a suitable route. At the end of the expedition, these pioneers envisioned arriving in Oregon City. If this exploratory mission failed, they would have to retrace their steps to The Dalles and take to the river in boats. There was determination to reach their destination for it was late in the season and what money had been left after the overland trip had very nearly all been spent on the present venture. If a retreat to The Dalles had to be undertaken, the pioneers would have arrived without funds any with little hope of getting settled in the Willamette Valley that year.

Barlow led his small wagon train in a southerly direction to avoid the foothills of the great "Mountain Hood." After about 30 miles he found himself in Tygh Valley where there was a trail that headed into the west over a shoulder of the mountain.

First there was Sam Barlow and his entourage which included his son William, age 22. They were joined by Joel Palmer with 23 wagons and fifteen families. William Henry Rector had also arrived at The Dalles in the fall of 1845. At Wascopam Methodist Mission (established in 1838), the earlier name for The Dalles, he met the Rev. Alvin F. Waller, the superintendent. In a discussion about the lack of a formal wagon route from The Dalles to Oregon City, Rev. Waller advocated Rector try going south to look for a pass between the mountains. He also said that some others had gone on ahead a few days earlier by this route. Rector apparently believed that traveling in a larger company was indicated for he hurried along and in three days came to the camp of Barlow and Palmer.

The pioneering men over the route in the fall of 1845 as recorded in history were Sam Barlow, Henry Knighton. Joel

MEMO TO READERS:
    Over the years the route of the Barlow Road changed and is not exactly the same as it was in 1845. Some of it was lost to overgrowth, some lost due to erosion and in the lower stretches areas have been cultivated by farmers. Early maps, filed with the Assessor of Wasco County, show old routes that appear to agree with routes on sketch-maps of pioneers and appear to correlate with modern aerial photo-mapping. One older map in the archives of the Oregon Historical Society shows the approximate route for its whole length.

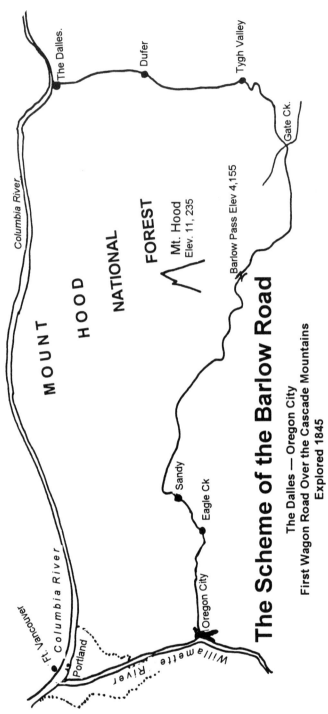

The Scheme of the Barlow Road

The Dalles — Oregon City
First Wagon Road Over the Cascade Mountains
Explored 1845

Highway 26 generally follows the western portion of the Barlow Road

16

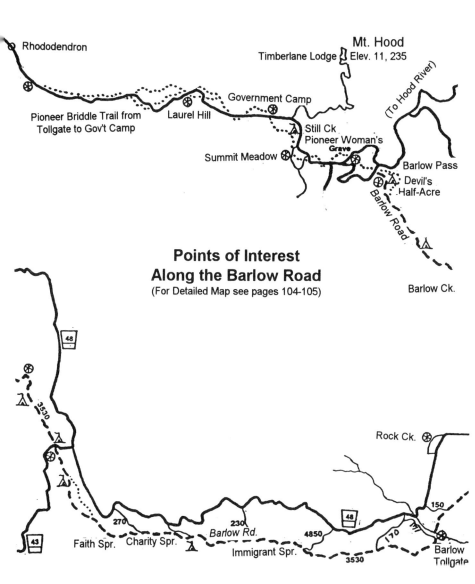

Rhododendron

Mt. Hood
Elev. 11, 235

Timberlane Lodge

(To Hood River)

Government Camp

Pioneer Briddle Trail from
Tollgate to Gov't Camp

Laurel Hill

Still Ck
Pioneer Woman's
Grave

Summit Meadow

Barlow Pass

Devil's
Half-Acre

Barlow Road

**Points of Interest
Along the Barlow Road**
(For Detailed Map see pages 104-105)

Barlow Ck.

48

3530

Rock Ck.

150

270

230

48

Barlow Rd.

4850

170

43

Faith Spr.

Charity Spr.

Immigrant Spr.

3530

Barlow
Tollgate

17

The route over the south flank of Mt. Hood was rugged and required trail-blazing before wagons could pass.

Palmer and William H. Rector. But these were only four. There were many more in the group including several women.

The evening of this linkup, Barlow and his companions who had been exploring the proposed route returned with news of a fine meadow beyond the crest of the trail. These scouts said it would be necessary to clear out the brush to make a trail wide enough to pass wagons. Palmer wrote:

October 4: This morning myself and companion, with a scanty supply of provisions for a two days' journey, started on a westerly course into the mountains. From the open ground we could see Mt. Hood. Our object was to go south and near this peak. For five miles the country [was] alternately prairie and yellow pine; we then ascended a ridge which ascended gradually to the west. This we followed ten miles. After the crossing of a little brushy bottom, we took over another ridge for four or five miles very heavily timbered and densely covered with undergrowth. We descended the ridge for a short distance and traveled a level bench for four miles, this is covered with very large and tall fir timber. We then descended the mountain traveling westward for one and a half miles and then came to a small branch which we named Rock Creek....

Palmer's journal continues in this manner with careful description of the land traversed. The following day he described the route as "abrupt and difficult." Satisfied that his wagons could make the transit, the pair of explorers returned to their base camp and prepared the people for the trip.

Before they could leave certain plans had to be evaluated and actions taken. The loose cattle would be dispatched with a party over the old cattle trail. Some men were sent back to The Dalles for extra food for the trip and would catch up. Some were to remain in the camp. Others would pack food for the trip and the remainder proceeded into the mountains to clear trail.

The distance between Oregon City and The Dalles by this route was estimated to be about 100 miles. Some would proclaim it was the most rugged, most difficult portion of the entire length of the Oregon Trail. They did not want to guess at the number of days it would take for the journey as the route was untested by wagons. An exploration hike was decided upon. Palmer recorded:

> On the morning of October 11th ... we took some provisions in our pockets, an axe and one rifle and started. We came to a cedar swamp so covered with heavy timber and brush that it was almost impossible to get through it. We were at least one hour in traveling half a mile.

Palmer described the scene when he turned and looked in the opposite direction:

> Stretching away to the south was a range of mountains which from the bottom appeared to be connected with the mountain on our left. It appeared to be covered with timber far up then a space of over two miles covered with grass then a space of more than a mile destitute of vegetation, then commenced the snow. The mountain continued to rise until the eye was pained in looking to the top.

Palmer had been seized by the magnificence of Oregon scenery. "To Him who is in love of nature holds communion with

---

*This comment seems subjective in view of the difficulties encountered by many who had either been forced to climb the Burnt River Canyon just west of the Snake River on the main Oregon Trail, or had been on the Stephen Meek "lost" wagon train in the Central Oregon desert. A large caravan had split at Fort Boise with some taking each route. Both sections arrived at The Dalles and faced the same challenges as Barlow and Palmer about the final route to Oregon City. For details about the Burnt River Canyon route see *Flagstaff Hill.* For a recently researched account of the Meek Wagon train see *The Search for Oregon's Lost Blue Bucket Mine; the Steven Meek Wagon Train of 1845.* Both books are identified in the bibliography.

> At one point he declared he saw Mount Hood in plain view—"I had never before looked upon a sight so nobly grand. We had previously seen only the top of it but now we had a view of the whole mountain. No pen can give an adequate description of this scene."

her visible forms" wrote William Cullen Bryant, "... lose thyself in the continuous woods where rolls the Oregon and hears no sound save his own dashings...."*

His party of three moved along climbing until the grass disappeared and they came to a ridge "entirely destitute of vegetation. About this time they metthe men who had started with the loose cattle. The rigors of mountain climbing and apparent inability to coral the cattle at night had taken its toll on the animals. About one-third had been lost but the drovers were encountered while they were searching for strays. The two parties teamed and proceeded to the cattlemen's camp on the west side of Mount Hood.

The route was badly broken with ridges, ravines, patches of snow until Palmer gasped when they came to "a deep kanyon or gulf cut out by the wash from the mountain above us—a precipitate cliff of rocks at the head prevented our passage around it.... I judged the ravine to be three thousand feet deep." Palmer was describing Zigzag Canyon through which runs the Zigzag River (see Map Point No. 23, pages 104-105):

> The manner of descending is to turn directly to the right, go zigzag for about one hundred yards then turn short around and go zigzag until you come under the place where you started from, then on to the right and so on until you reach the base. In the bottom is a stream filled with sand. After crossing, we ascended in the same manner, went around the point of the ridge where we struck another ravine the side of which were covered with grass and whortelberry bushes. In this ravine we found the camp of our friends.

Palmer explored various ways of continuing the exploring trip but was confronted with fatigue of his companions who wanted to find an easier route. Palmer, who was of a different mind, wanted to push on and did so. His words:

> I found that by climbing up a cliff of snow and ice about forty feet but not

---

* "The Thanatopsis," Wm. Cullen Bryant in *The Poetical Works of William Cullen Bryant* Roslyn Edition, p. 21-22 Appleton (1910)

Looking down Laurel Hill .

so steep but that by getting upon one cliff and cutting holes to stand in and hold on by, it could be ascended [so I] cut and carved my way up the cliff and when up to the top was forced to admit that it was something of an undertaking. My moccasins were worn out and the soles of my feet exposed to the snow.

> **When Mary Louisa Black traveled on the Barlow Road in 1865, she diaried that the experience was harrowing. Nearly everyone in the party was sick including Mary Louisa. They had stopped and arranged to have one ill person taken back then went on:**
>
> Those that we had left tried to get the wagons up [the hill] with the assistance of some men traveling in a light 2-horse vehicle. On the third drive [attempt] our wagon got nearly to the top of a short stoop turn in he road and stopped. The wagon commenced running backward. I called to the inexperienced [helper] to hold the wheel but he kept beating the horses till they became unmanageable and the wagon went off the road. We then tried to hold it by grabbing the fore wheel. The man that was driving [the wagon] behind [us] jumped down from his seat hollering for those within to get out and he just got to the hind wheel in time to save the wagon. I made all haste I could to get the children out. It then took all hands to get the wagon back on the road.
>
> —The Oregon & Overland Trail Diary of Mary Louisa Black in 1865.
> (Webb Research Group 1989 p. 59)

View of Laurel Hill. The hill was steep, had loose rock, was difficult to descend and downright dangerous.

Rope burns on stumps of trees remain as mute evidence of disaster-prone Laurel Hill where ropes were wound around trees in effort to ease wagons down the hill.

so steep but that by getting upon one cliff and cutting holes to stand in and hold on by, it could be ascended [so I] cut and carved my way up the cliff and when up to the top was forced to admit that it was something of an undertaking. My moccasins were worn out and the soles of my feet exposed to the snow.

Rope burn on stump, Laurel Hill.

Recent view of Barlow Road near Summit Meadow.
This area is within Mt. Hood National Forest.

Barlow Road's ruggedness softens as it nears
Oregon City.

25

On returning to the trail he met his two companions who had not followed him over the snow and ice ridge. After a few miles they came to another river, the Sandy River (see Map Point No. 27). Palmer was of the opinion that wagons could pass safely.

From his diary:

> The day was getting far advanced and we had no provisions save each of us had a small biscuit, and knowing we had at least 25 miles to travel before reaching those who were working on the road I hastened down the mountain.... On our way we came to a beautiful spring of water surrounded by fine timber and the ground covered with whortelberry* bushes many of them hanging full of fruit. We halted, ate our biscuits, gathered berries then proceeded down the mountain.... When we got to the bottom and arrived in camp about eleven o'clock at night—and although not often tired, I was willing to acknowledge that I was near being so. I certainly was hungry but my condition was so much better than that of my two friends....
>
> On the morning of the 13th, we held a consultation and determined upon the future movements of the company. The party designated to bring us provisions had performed that service but the amount of our provisions was nearly exhausted and many of the party had no means of procuring more. Some of them began to despair getting through [to Oregon City] this season. Those left with the camp were unable to keep the cattle together and a number of them [cattle] had been lost. The Indians had stolen several horses and a variety of mishaps occurred....

It was impossible to keep more than one third of the men working on the road as the remainder were needed to attend the camp and pack provisions.

After considerably more hiking, exploring and wandering looking for the best route, the party arrived in Oregon City. Thus was the travail of spending a month breaking through the Cascades. Their route was calculated to have been 160 miles with Palmer writing: "The travel will be much shortened by giving direct course, bridging the streams, and upon ground [more] favorable for a good road."

In 1846, Samuel Barlow retraced his route and was granted a permit by the territorial legislature to built a toll road. This road ran between Tygh Valley and Sandy. Those who wanted the right to pass were to be charged $5.00 for a team plus one dollar for each man, woman and head of cattle. But most who used it, and

---

*Probably huckleberries which are common on Mt. Hood and account for many excellent home-made pies every fall. Bears eat them too but Palmer does not mention countering any bears.

Tollgate No. 5 about 1880 on the Barlow Road.

over time this amounted to thousands, had no money so the venture did not prove successful. Many years later there was a rebuilding project conducted by the Barlow and Mt. Hood Road Company. But the original 1845 route was on the *north* side of the Sandy River and this venture pushed their route along the south side. This has caused some confusion among some writers.

A businessman, Henry Wemme, bought the Barlow Road in 1912. He wanted to finish it for automobiles. But in 1919 he gave it to the State of Oregon and much of it is today's Highway 26. ❖

Oregon City in 1874. View faces south. The Mc-Loughlin House is hidden in trees. Compare with picture on page 9. Note railroad below bluff.

Chapter 2
Dr. John McLoughlin, Father of Oregon City

Workers under the direction of Dr. John McLoughlin, Chief Factor of the Hudson's Bay Company at Fort Vancouver, put up some log cabins at the falls of the Willamette River in 1829. These were the first whites to see the falls, the ultimate site of Oregon City, although Indians had lived there for thousands of years.

McLoughlin was a Canadian, of Scottish, Irish and French descent born in 1784 at Riviere du Loup. He was therefore a British subject. At the age of 14 he apprenticed himself to a medical doctor in Quebec to become a physician and completed his study then was licensed as a doctor before his 19th birthday. For the rest of his life he was known far and wide as "Doctor" McLoughlin.

His first job was at Fort William on Lake Superior for the British owned Northwest Company as an assistant to the regular physician. But he became interested in the fur trading business and became a chief trader for the company. On this assignment he traveled to other posts while the trappers and their families were in winter quarters. Later he became a wintering partner and was placed in charge of posts that were supply centers as well as trading posts. In 1814 be became a partner in the company.

After the merger of the Northwest Company and the Hudson's Bay Company in 1821, McLoughlin, with 18 years in the fur trade, was appointed "Chief Factor" (president) and was transfered back to his old post at Fort William.

He became Chief Factor of he Columbia Department* in the Oregon Country in June 1824 and left for that district the following month. His wife and two young children went with him as this was considered a permanent assignment.

---

*The Columbia Dept. extended from the Russian settlements on the north to those of the Spanish on the south an from the Pacific Ocean to the crest of the Rocky Mountains—the entire Pacific Northwest.

Dr. John McLoughlin at an early age. Said to be his favorite painting of himself.

McLoughlin was physically fit for a rugged life in the wilds. He stood six feet four inches tall and of a stocky build. Although he started with blonde hair, family legend tells that following a serious boating accident, at age 32, his hair turned snow white. The Indians called him "White-Headed Eagle." He had somewhat of a bland, courteous manner about himself—dignified—with a prematurely gray head of bushy hair framing a pleasant face with kindly blue eyes that could become icy when his temper flared.

His trip to the west was across Canada by canoe portaging

The McLoughlin home on Main Street, Oregon City. In 1909 it was saved by the McLoughlin Memorial Association and moved to present site above the bluff.

when necessary. The troupe used horses for moving their goods over the Rocky Mountains then it was back to the canoes for the final drift down the Columbia River.

The destination was Fort George at the mouth of the Columbia River.*

Dr. McLoughlin was expected to rule his territory for the best interests of his company and keep peace with the Indians so the fur business would not be interrupted. He did both. Then he was challenged, nearly invaded with unanticipated visitors, first a few then many—Americans!

He was known as friendly *hyas tyee* ("Good Chief") by the Indians and he was often called on to be "doctor-in-fact" to pioneers and missionaries who would arrive at his doorstep, Fort Vancouver, in poor health, hungry and destitute. He provided the Americans with thousands of dollars worth of goods on their personal I.O.U.'s at Fort Vancouver and later from his store in Oregon City. As the "head man" of his district he was hounded from all sides by all sorts of requests and still had to maintain a stern hold on his subordinates for the benefit of the business. The

---

* Fort George was the name given to Fort Astoria in 1813 when the British took control of it in "an act of war" due to some unfortunate circumstances for the Americans who had been there first. The site was returned to the Americans by the Treaty of Ghent in 1814 then renamed Fort Astoria. A good description of this is in Winther and in Johansen and Gates.

McLoughlin House, a National Historic Site on Center Street in Oregon City. It, and adjacent Barclay House, is open to visitors usually daily except Monday.

fur trade was good, but eventually declined so there was a vast agricultural undertaking as well as trade with the Russians also under his direction. Historians report he had a nervous stomach, today called prone to ulcers, probably due to all the stress.

His headquarters was the hub of all British activity in the northwest. As an example of the extremes to which he became involved, he arranged ransom with Indians along the northwest coast, of what later became Washington, for three shipwrecked nearly dead Japanese sailors.*

Dr. McLoughlin had to keep abreast of all American activities which not only included the Jason Lee missionary party of 1834, but incursions on his domain by Americans by sea. During

---

*The amazing details about these waifs, including the fact that, having been rescued and brought to Fort Vancouver, they were taught in the British school by an *American* teacher, Cyrus Shepard a Methodist missionary, is in *Wrecked Japanese Junks Adrift in the North Pacific Ocean* by Bert Webber. See bibliography.

Dr. John McLoughlin

1829-1830, there were six American sea captains trading with the Indians for furs and paying a better price. To McLoughlin's chagrin, the sailors loaded the Indians with rum!

As we have seen, McLoughlin investigated the harnessing of water power from the falls of the Willamette in 1829 when he built a mill race and some cabins. Apparently the Indians didn't like his presence, so they burned down the cabins. When Jason Lee showed up, the good doctor hastened him off to the south of the Columbia some say on the presumption that when the international border was drawn it would be the Columbia River as the obvious point of separation. If this came to be, Lee and his Americans would not be within the British "sector."

To protect his interests at the falls, McLoughlin, at first friendly to Rev. Waller who showed up to stake a claim for the Methodists, set about plating the village and named it Oregon City.

Dr. McLoughlin's used this desk at Fort Vancouver. It is now exhibited in McLoughlin House in Oregon City.

By 1845 the Hudson's Bay Company became agitated with McLoughlin for all his help to the Americans and felt he was no longer representing the company's best interest thus he was forced to resign. At age 61, he retired to his land at Oregon City. He denounced his British citizenship and on being encouraged to do so, he applied for American citizenship in 1849. This was granted after the usual two year wait, in 1851. (It is interesting to learn that although he was not yet a naturalized American, he was allowed to vote.)

Under the Donation Land Law of 1850, Americans staked claims on his land and took it from him but he was allowed to keep his home and his business.

Dr. McLoughlin came from a mixed-religious background. His father was Roman Catholic and his mother was Protestant. His maternal grandfather offered to pay for his education but only if he was raised as a Protestant. For whatever reason, McLoughlin returned to the Catholic Church in 1842.

He was married twice, first to an Indian girl of the Red River tribe who died shortly after she gave birth to their son Joseph. Then be married Marguerite Wadin McKay, a Cree Indian. Into the union she brought four children from her first marriage. With McLoughlin's son, Joseph, and Marguerite's four, this was only a start for he and Marguerite had four more—two boys and two girls. He was directly responsible for eight of the nine children, and took his position as head of the family very seriously and decided early that all would be educated. As Chief Factor of Hudson's Bay Company's post at Fort Vancouver, he set up a school and provided teachers. This was the first school in the Pacific Northwest. Cyrus Shepard, of the Methodist Mission, was one of several teachers.

McLoughlin died on September 3, 1857, at the age of 73, in the parlor of his home.

Some of Dr. John McLoughlin's experiences in Oregon City are included in chapter 2. ❖

Chapter 3
The Beginnings of Oregon City

There are a number of ideas expressed by writers as to how Oregon got its name. Probably the earliest appears to have been with Major Robert Rogers, of Massachusetts, who served the English during the French and Indian Wars. He was aware of explorations of the French into the interior of Canada and as far south as Illinois. He wrote to King George III seeking a commission for heading an expedition of exploration to the west. In support of his request, he included a report of the journeys of the French who said Indians knew of a river they called *"Ouragon."*

A fellow who worked with Rogers, Jonathan Carver, claimed there was "the River Oregon, or the River of the West that falls into the Pacific Ocean at the Strait of Anin." Carver appears to have been the first to use the spelling as known today.

Johnson and Gates point out: "Today both Rogers and Carver are remembered chiefly because they were the first to use the name Oregon [that was] later to be applied to the whole Pacific Northwest."*

General histories identify various explorers who trekked the country or floated down rivers to the Pacific Ocean and some who arrived on the Oregon coast by ship. The most popular were those in the Lewis and Clark Expedition 1804-1806 and in the Wilson Price Hunt Expedition 1810-1812—the Astorians.

Due to an interest in religion and the knowledge there were Indians who had not been converted to Christianity in the far west, missionary societies formed to send teachers and preachers there. When an article appeared in the *Christian Advocate and Journal* in 1832 about four Indians who had gone to St. Louis seeking the "whiteman's book of Heaven," it was the impetus for action.

Reverend Jason Lee and his nephew Rev. Daniel Lee, were

---

*Rogers does not seem to be remembered in Oregon history by having a mountain or other place named for him but there is Carver Glacier named for Jonathan Carver. It is on the north slope of South Sister in Deschutes County. See Chapter 1 about Wm. Cullen Bryant's contribution to the matter of Oregon's name.

approved by the Mission Society of the Methodist Episcopal Church at the New England June 1833 conference to establish a mission in the west. These men, along with helpers Philip L. Edwards, Cyrus Shepard and Courtney M. Walker, arranged to make the trip as part of the Nathaniel J. Wyeth Expedition the next spring.

At this time the destination for travelers was Fort Vancouver on the Columbia River. Their host there was Dr. John McLoughlin, Chief Factor of the Hudson's Bay Company, who welcomed them and saw to their personal needs. (He did this for most all passersby, a few of whom stayed for months.) While there, Lee preached regularly to the congregation at the fort apparently with agreement from Dr. McLoughlin that he do so.

Some would have it that McLoughlin was preserving the land north of the Columbia River for English interests so pushed for the Lees to start their work on the Willamette River which was south of the Columbia. But a more apparent reason for the forming of what became the Willamette Mission in that valley was the better ground for growing life-sustaining crops than was found in the Vancouver area. McLoughlin, in promoting settlement in the valley-to-the-south for newcomers, was in fact "decentralizing" a potential impact of too many people and too great a drain on the Hudson's Bay Company immediate resources at Fort Vancouver.

After getting settled to the extent possible, Jason Lee seemed captivated with the potential for American colonization in the Willamette Valley. He wrote to the Mission Board that his location was in:

a central position from whence missionary labors may be extended in almost every direction among natives and those emigrants who may hereafter settle in that vast and fertile territory.

His plot of ground was about ten miles north of Salem.

Just two years later the Mission Board sent 13 helpers, including Dr. Elijah White. With this additional force, Lee established a mission at Wascopam (The Dalles) on the Columbia River in 1838 as well as other mission stations. It had been determined there was a substantial Indian population at The Dalles when compared to the number of Indians to be

Wascopam (The Dalles) Mission

"Christianized" at the Willamette site. But the latter was much more suitable for farming and was becoming the heart of a new settlement of whites from the east.

In June 1840, Rev. Alvin F. Waller was dispatched with a party to establish a mission and a store at Willamette Falls. There seems to have been a dual-purpose for this event. One was said to be for missionary work among the Indians while the other was to attempt to gain a foothold there in the face of Dr. McLoughlin's interests (established in 1829) for developing water-power. In short, as historian William D. Welsh put it,

> Waller established squatters rights on the land and using the doctor's logs, built a branch mission. McLoughlin did not object seriously to this infringement of his rights but gave notice to Rev. Waller that he was welcome to build there but that McLoughlin was not relinquishing his claim to the building or the ground

McLoughlin's prior claim was very clear for he had established a mill-race and constructed some log cabins there which Indians burned. McLoughlin's men had prepared timbers for building a house—the cut logs Waller purloined.* The ever

*Walsh mentions that McLoughlin sent a letter about this to Waller's boss, Jason Lee, but the authors, in an effort to find it, searched McLoughlin's correspondence but found no mention about his 1829 enterprise at the falls of the Willamette River.

38

friendly McLoughlin allowed Waller to use his timbers already pre-cut for construction so Waller could assemble his own building in less time than to start by having to select trees and cut them down. This project resulted in a building made up of two apartments one of which, for the time, being would be a warehouse for mission goods. George Abernethy was appointed the storekeeper.

> In June 1840, after preparing some dried apples for cooking, Mrs. Waller tossed the seeds out of doors. One sprouted thus the first apple tree in what would become Oregon City grew in the lot where the Methodist Church was first built.

It appears that the first buildings at Willamette Falls, later named Oregon City, were those of Dr. John McLoughlin—the cabins the Indians had burned—then the Waller building.

There followed several years of frustrations for both Waller and McLoughlin because the latter was now seeing that the Methodists had more in mind than mere missionary work among the Indians. In fact, Waller seemed to be making every effort to "take over" the property earlier claimed by McLoughlin in a manner described by Bancroft as "Waller's Wickedness."* By 1842 the claim-jumper Waller had a small sawmill operating and was planning his flour mill. When push came to shove through the Oregon Land Bill of 1850, Dr. McLoughlin lost all of his rights. As these issues are beyond the scope of this book, we invite interested readers to pursue the listings in the bibliography for details.

Waller, in 1841, established the Island Milling Company for the purpose of making flour to sell in Hawaii. The joint stock company was set up with three-fourths of the members belonging to the mission and the remainder were settlers. The outsiders — settlers — were allowed so it could be said the business was of a public nature and not a missionary enterprise. Had this been true, far better sites for a mill would have been well upstream some thirty to forty miles. (There arises a report the flour mill might not have engaged in the export business for in 1843 Johansen and

---

* Bancroft Vol. I page 205

Gates point out that Hudson's Bay "Company was the sole purchaser of the wheat crop...[and] made immense profits [by selling] to the Russians in Alaska and to the Hawaiian Islands. p.240)

In the fall of 1842, Island Milling Company set up a saw mill on the island part of McLaughlin's 1829 claim. To try to protect his interests, McLoughlin immediately built a saw mill nearby and notified Waller of his intent to also put up a grist mill there. In that year McLoughlin, in a further effort to stake his claim in the area, also laid out and named the growing village "Oregon City." (At about this time there were perhaps 150 Americans in Oregon but every year from that time on, emigrants from the United States expanded the roll. These were largely congregated between today's Salem and Oregon City.)

The milling company continued to expand on the island part of McLoughlin's claim while the principal plotters of the Mission, Abernethy, Waller and others, still resided on the site of the town.

In 1843, the Methodist Church was erected and in the fall a large number—about 2,000—of immigrants arrived from the overland trek; many of them as families some of which took up building properties in the new town.

The upstart village of Oregon City, that was growing every year, boasted 75 buildings in 1844.

With all of these people came a need for government as the federal government in Washington D.C. had no force in the Oregon Country. This was because this great area in the west was not within the United States. After considerable debate and several attempts, a provisional government was formed in May 1843 at Champoeg (also spelled Champoag in some sources), near Salem. But it hardly functioned for it had power only over Americans in a population of many French-Canadians and Indians as well as British. It would operate only until a permanent government could be set up which happened in the spring of 1845 when George Abernathy, the mission storekeeper at the falls of the Willamette River, was appointed governor.

There was much dispute in English circles about the earlier actions of Dr. McLoughlin and his handling of Americans who came to Fort Vancouver often destitute and in need of help. He felt he was being spied upon by some of his Company's key

MAP

)REGON CITY

Original map, Oregon City. (Details on page 42)

people. In addition, American settlers were staking claims on what had traditionally been recognized as Company property. In one case, McLoughlin had to appeal to the Provisional Government for relief—which he got. But the tenure of the Grand Company in northwest America was about to come to an end with the formation of the Provisional Government. The Hudson's Bay Company could see the writing on the wall and decided to sell out.

Settlement of an amount of money the United States would pay did not come about until the 1860's. In the meanwhile the good doctor, sometimes called the "White Headed Eagle" because of his crop of snow-white hair and his awesome power, placed all property of Hudson's Bay Company under the control of the Provisional Government of Oregon and resigned his position in August of 1845. He took up permanent residence on his land in Oregon City the following spring.

The fortunes of Lee's Willamette Mission ran out when Lee was dismissed and the mission properties ordered sold. When Waller was no longer required to hold any part of the Oregon City claim, he was assigned to the mission at The Dalles This appointment did not last and he returned to the Willamette Valley.

Plausibly the greatest achievement of the Methodists, in addition to establishing an American as the first "resident" at what would become Oregon City, was the founding of a school that became Willamette University.

Oregon City had been founded in 1842. Oregon Territory was created on August 14, 1848. Oregon statehood occurred on February 14, 1859. ❖

41

Map and Plan of Oregon City

This plat is on a scale of two hundred and forty feet to the inch. So much of the town as lies between Washington Street and the River was surveyed in the spring of 1844 by Jesse Applegate. The remainder of the town from Blocks numbered ninety three (93) to one hundred and seventy nine (179) inclusive was surveyed by Robert R. Short in the Autumn of 1849. All streets except 6th Street are 60 feet wide and cross each other at right angles. 6th Street is sixty feet wide on the hill or bluff and at the River, but is only about 30 feet wide at the foot of the Bluff. All lots in that part of town surveyed by Jesse Applegate are at least 66 feet front and 100 feet back. The alleys in this part of town are ten feet wide. Fractions of lots are marked on the plot. All lots in that part of town surveyed by Robert R. Short are 60 feet front and 105 feet back. The alleys in this part of town are twenty-six feet wide. Blocks 96, 40, 102 and 152 are public squares. That part of the town set apart by red lines has been donated to the Probate Judges of Clackamas County in trust and upon conditions specified in the deed conveying it. Some lots are more than 60 feet front in consequence of an allowance made because of difficulty of measuring the Block, being in some instances made more than full. The space between the edge of the Bluff and the Blocks numbered 33, 32, 31, 30, 73, 74, 75 and 76 is donated for a promenade for the inhabitants of Oregon City. All the space in front of the Blocks on water streets now covered by the width of the street (sixty feet) is reserved as private property. All the space between the edge of the Bluff along in front of Blocks numbered 73, 74, 75, 76 and 77 is reserved as private property . The place beginning for that part of the town which lies immediately along the River and under the Bluff is at the North East corner of Block number (1) one marked on the plot, the land mark being a black hewed stone placed in the ground at the place designated. The streets in this portion of the town parallel with the River from the Southern end of the Block numbered (1) to the Northern end of the block numbered four (4), bear North 35' 30" east from Block numbered five (5) to Block number nine (9), they bear north 55' East. The place of beginning for that portion of the town lying on the hill or back of the Bluff is at the North West corner of Block numbered (37) thirty seven (now owned by Judge Thornton) distinguished by a black hewed stone placed in the ground. Streets on this part of the town parallel with the River bear North 34' East. All streets, alleys and squares are donated to the City Corporation for the public, the streets to be forever kept open, the squares to be enclosed if deemed expedient. All ferry rights are reserved along the entire front of the town.

John McLoughlin

OREGON TERRITORY)
Clackamas County   ) ss

Be it remembered that on this second day of December in the year of our Lord one thousand and eight hundred and fifty, personally appeared before me, Francis S. Holland, Clerk of the Probate Court of Clackamas County in Oregon Territory, the above named John McLoughlin, with whom I am personally acquainted and acknowledged the signing of the above foregoing instrument accompanying the town plat of Oregon City for the purpose therein mentioned.

Witness my hand and the seal of my office, the day and year above written.

Francis S. Holland
Clerk of the Probate Court of Clackamas County

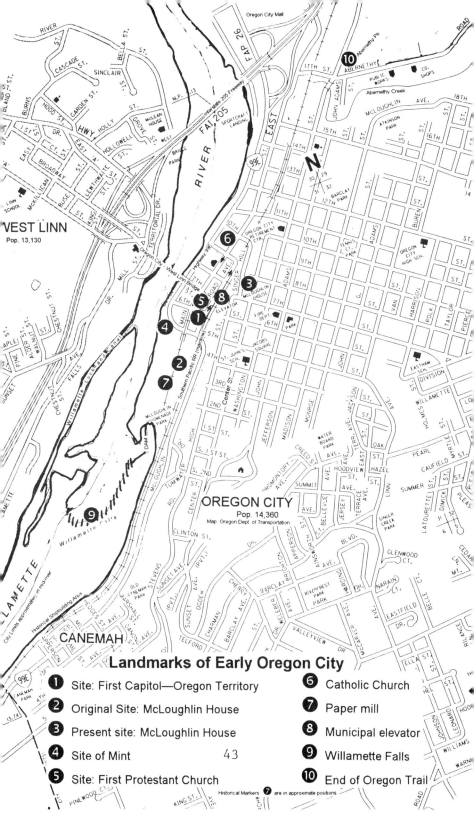

Landmarks of Early Oregon City

1 Site: First Capitol—Oregon Territory

2 Original Site: McLoughlin House

3 Present site: McLoughlin House

4 Site of Mint

5 Site: First Protestant Church

6 Catholic Church

7 Paper mill

8 Municipal elevator

9 Willamette Falls

10 End of Oregon Trail

43

Historical Markers **7** are in approximate positions

Early Historical Facts About Oregon City

1829   Dr. John McLoughlin claimed land, built cabins at the site of Oregon City for Hudson's Bay Company

1840   Methodist minister Alvin F. Waller establishes branch mission and store; first fruit trees (apple) planted

1841   First grist mill in Willamette Valley

1842   First saw mill in Willamette valley; first planting of vegetable garden – potatoes; first novel, *The Prairie Flower*, written in Oregon by Sidney Walter Moss; estab. of first public library in Oregon

1843   First Provisional Legislative session convened May 16 at the Methodist Mission granary, this first legislative hall on the Pacific Coast was provided gratis by the Mission; first Protestant church building erected west of the Missouri River (Methodist); first public primary school in Oregon; first hotel in Oregon; first Oregon debating society formed

1844   First community west of Rocky Mountains incorporated by the Provisional Legislature; first jail in Oregon erected on property donated by Dr. McLoughlin

1846   *Oregon Spectator,* first newspaper founded west of Missouri River appeared February 5; first Masonic Lodge west of the Missouri River founded Feb. 21; first Roman Catholic province in Oregon Territory established; first toll road charter granted (for Barlow Rd.)

1847   First post office in Willamette Valley March 29; first book store in Oregon Terr.; first book printed in English on the Pacific Coast

1848   First ministerial association formed by Congregational and Presbyterian ministers west of Rocky Mountains

1849   On March 31, designated capital of Oregon Territory; first territorial government met July 16; first mint in Oregon minted $5 and $10 gold "beaver" pieces—about $55,000

1850   First Federal Court and Land Office on Pacific Coast accepts and records plat of City of San Francisco;

1855   first telegraph message in Oregon originated, sent to Portland

1861   First Oregon State Fair

1866   First paper mill on Pacific Coast erected;

1889   First long distance commercial transport of electric power in the United States produced the power for 55 electric street lights in Portland.

1893   First electric interurban railroad in U.S. runs between Oregon City and Portland.

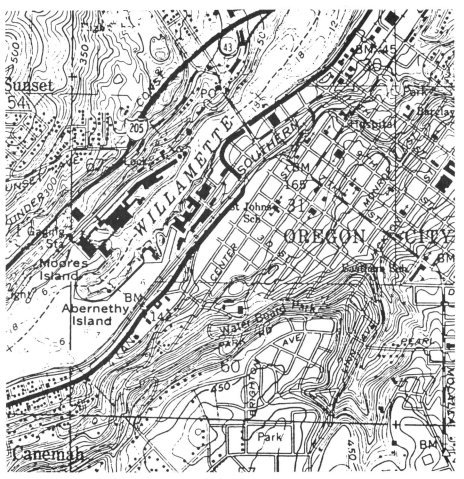

Contour map of Oregon City. For city streets see map on page 43 and aerial photographs on pages 106-107. Main and 6th Streets (lower) in 1885. Compare growth of telephone poles on p. 79.

Chapter 4
Indian Trouble at Oregon City

There had been an exchange of shots between Indians and whites on March 4, 1844 at Oregon City which led to the formation of the first volunteer company of riflemen in Oregon on March 9.

The "serious trouble" as Bancroft phrased it, had been brought about by a quarrel between "Negro Winslow and the Molallas." This was George Winslow, a negro, also known as Winslow Anderson.

The Indians had become unusually surly as a result of a quarrel between an Indian named Comstock, and Winslow over a business deal. To obtain redress from Winslow, so the story goes, Comstock, who was known to be "bold and vicious," vowed vengeance and appropriated a horse belonging to Winslow. Dr. Elisha White, the Indian Agent, forced Comstock to give it back so Comstock set out after Winslow and another Negro, James D. Saules, who was in some way also involved.

Saules complained about the matter to White who immediately posted a $200 reward for the capture of Comstock with the intention of shipping him to the Cayuse and Nez Perces for trial according to their laws. But this upset Comstock to the point where he and some buddies, dressed in war paint, roared into Oregon City openly demonstrating hostility. Bancroft says this is that happened:

> After creating an alarm, he crossed the river to a village in search of recruits [then] shortly afterward reappeared on the Oregon City side. His landing was opposed by a confused crowd of white men who, without a leader ... [tried] to capture him, some for the reward and others with a more deadly purpose. Fire-arms were discharged on both sides simultaneously. In the melee, Comstock was killed and three [whites were] wounded.

Two of the whites, a Mr. Rogers and George W. LeBreton, a public figure, died of their wounds. A meeting was held to consider the matter with the result of the founding of the Oregon Rangers, the first military unit in Oregon Territory.*

---

*Members of the Oregon Rangers are listed by name as well as the details of the meeting.. See: *Oregon Archives* MS., 10, 12; Bancroft I: 280-285.

The fact that a militia had been formed appears to have
settled tempers on both sides but there is no evidence that the
riflemen were actually called out. When the excitement died over
time, and all the circumstances became known, is was apparent
that the whole affair might have been avoided had each side
exercised moderation.

Comstock's relatives were pacified by a handout of new
blankets to his widow by Dr. McLoughlin on Indian Agent
White's request.

There is some evidence that the formation of the Rangers
filled a dual purpose for the Provisional government. One was to
assert itself for law and order while the second reason was to
serve notice on Dr. McLoughlin that the Americans were no
longer dependent on the Hudson's Bay Company's previous one-
handed control over all the area.

But what of Winslow and Saules? An account by Anderson
tells a slightly different story. In that account the Indians only
"planned" an attack. In a meeting with the Indian Agent, both
sides present, "Winslow, on seeing Comstock make a sudden
movement, chose to interpret it as he meant to shoot someone so
he [Winslow] shot him." Anderson does not mention the Oregon
Rangers or the payoff in blankets but says that Winslow left town
and resettled "near the mouth of the Columbia River."

Saules stayed in Oregon City for awhile and was arrested
after making threats against Charles E. Picket. Because the jail
had not yet been built, Saules was urged to leave town which he
did moving first to Cathlemet then to the Methodist mission at
Clatsop Plains. ❖

CITY ORDINANCE.

OREGON CITY CORPORATION.

Be it ordained and established by the Mayor and Trustees of Oregon City, in Council assembled:

1. That a City tax for 1846, of one-half per centum, be, and the same is hereby levied, for Corporation purposes, on all property subject to taxation, within the limits of said City.

2. That all alleys within the limits of said City, running parallel with Main and Water streets, be and the same are hereby closed, and all owners of lots adjoining such alleys, shall be entitled to the use of the same, each in their proper proportions respectively.

3. That from and after the first day of April, 1846, all owners of swine, be and they are hereby prohibited from suffering the same to run at large within the limits of said City, under a penalty of not less than two nor more than ten dollars for each and every such offence, and in case any swine shall be found running at large contrary to the provision of this ordinance, it shall be the duty of the City Marshal to place the same in the public pound, and give immediate public notice thereof, by posting up a description of the same, in three of the most public places in said City, and unless claimed by the proper owner, and all charges paid, within fourteen days thereafter, such swine shall be publicly sold to the highest bidder, and the proceeds thereof paid over to the City Treasurer.

4. That all persons are hereby prohibited from discharging fire-arms during the night time, and on Sunday, within the limits of said City, under a penalty of not less than one nor more than ten dollars for each and every such offence.

5. That all persons are hereby prohibited from hauling logs or timber along the streets of said City, unless the same be attached to, or slung on wheels, under a penalty of not less than one nor more than ten dollars for each and every such offence.

6. That all persons are hereby prohibited from riding or driving furiously along the streets of said City, to the danger of the citizens, under a penalty of not less than two nor more than ten dollars for each and every such offence.

7. That any person found intoxicated, acting in a disorderly manner, or otherwise offending public decency within the limits of said City, shall be subject to a fine of not less than three nor more than ten dollars for each and every such offence.

A. LAWRENCE LOVEJOY, *Mayor.*

Attest: FRED. PRIGG, *City Recorder.*

February 23, 1846.

48

NELSON & McDONALD,

HAVING rented H. Burns' old stand in Multnomah City, on the west side of the Willamette river, are now ready to supply their friends and customers with all kinds of manufactured iron and steel. They have a large stock of assorted iron and steel on hand, which will enable them to supply all orders in their line with despatch. They have now on hand a number of Diamond Cary Plows of the best quality, axes, drawing knives, mortising chisels, and edge tools of all kinds, warranted to carry a good edge, or no charge. All of which will be sold at a moderate price for good pay.

Customers coming from the east side of the Willamette river to our shop for iron work, will be ferried free of charge.   Feb. 19, 1846—1tf

Administrator's Notice.

ALL persons indebted to the estate of George W. Le Breton, deceased, are hereby requested to make immediate payment to the subscriber.
JNO. H. COUCH, Adm'r.
Oregon City, Feb. 19, 1846—2tf

Mail Contracts to Let.

SEALED PROPOSALS will be received at the office of the postmaster general, in Oregon City, until the 20th inst., for carrying the mail on the following routes:

Route No. 1.—From Oregon City to Fort Vancouver, once in two weeks, by water.

Route No. 2.—From Oregon City to Hill's, in Twality county; thence to A. J. Hembree's, in Yam Hill county; thence to Andrew Smith's, Yam Hill county; thence to N. Ford's, Polk county; thence to Oregon Institute, Champoeg county; thence to Catholic Mission and Champoeg to Oregon City, once in two weeks, on horse back.

The contractor will enter into bond and security, to be approved of by the postmaster general.
W. G. T'VAULT, P. M. Gen.
Oregon City, Feb. 5, 1846.

A. Lawrence Lovejoy,
Attorney and Counsellor at Law and Solicitor in Chancery.

WILL practice in the Supreme and Criminal Courts of Oregon territory, and in the several County Courts.

Office, corner of Main and Second streets.
Oregon City, Jan. 20, 1846.   1y1

NOTICE.

THE subscribers have purchased out the stock of the Oregon Milling Company, and all the interest of the stockholders in the Island mills. They will, hereafter, carry on the business of the mills in partnership, under the name of the "Oregon Milling Company." Orders for lumber and lath will be filled with despatch. The flouring mill is now fitted up for manufacturing flour suitable for exportation.
Terms of grinding made known at the mill.
GEO. ABERNETHY,
ALANSON BEERS.
Oregon City, January 28, 1846—1tf

Administrator's Notice.

ALL persons indebted to the estate of Ewing Young, late of Yam Hill, deceased, are hereby notified to make immediate payment, and thereby save cost, as this is the last call, said estate having been ordered to be immediately closed up.
A. LAWRENCE LOVEJOY, Adm'r.
February 2, 1846-3w1

NOTICE.

I HAVE in store one box of medicine, shipped by Dr. Wm. B. Moffatt of New York, per barque Toulon, and consigned to Mr. John B. Rutter, Astoria. As I can learn nothing of Mr. Rutter, if said box is not claimed in two months from this date, it will be sold for charges. Any proceeds arising from same, after paying charges, will be remitted to the shipper.
F. W. PETTYGROVE.
Oregon City, Jan. 29, 1846.   3w1

NOTICE.

THE subscribers having fitted up their flouring mills for the purpose of manufacturing flour for exportation, will be unable to grind grists for toll, the length of the bolt and the apparatus for cooling flour, previous to bolting, contains so large a quantity, that a small grist would hardly commence falling into the flour chest before the hopper would be empty, consequently, if the grist should be white wheat, and spring wheat have been ground previous to the grist being put in the hopper, the person bringing the white wheat would get the flour of spring wheat. We will, therefore, hereafter grind on the following terms: For every bushel of merchantable wheat, measured in the Winchester or Territorial bushel, thirty-six pounds of flour will be given in exchange. If measured in the Imperial or Vancouver measure, forty pounds of flour will be given. In all cases the flour of fall wheat will be given in exchange for fall wheat; and the flour of spring wheat for spring wheat. No wheat will be ground on any terms that is not merchantable.
GEO. ABERNETHY,
ALANSON BEERS.
Oregon City, Feb. 2, 1846-1tf

Town Lots for Sale.

THE subscriber will offer for sale in a few days, a number of lots, situated on the lower part of his claim, lying on the Willamette river, and just at the foot of the Clackamas rapids. As the eligibility of this site for a town, has been attested by nearly all nautical men who have visited the river, and particularly by those navigating it during the summer season, it will be unnecessary to say any thing farther in its favour. The situation of the ground is dry, level, and at least ten feet above the highest water mark; and from it to the crossing of the Clackamas, where a bridge will be built the coming season, an almost level road may be opened.
C. E. PICKETT,
City Hotel, Oregon City.
Febuary 5, 1846-3t1

TO PERSONS WISHING TO SEND LETTERS EAST.

The postmaster general has contracted with Mr. H. Burns to carry the mail from Oregon City to Weston, in Missouri, for one trip only. Letters mailed at any of the offices, post paid, will be forwarded to any part of the United States. As the mail sent east, by Mr. Burns, will reach Weston early in the season, it would be advisable for those wishing to correspond with their friends in the east, to avail themselves of this opportunity. Postage only fifty cents on single sheets.

TIMES OF HOLDING COURTS.

The regular sessions of the Supreme Court will be held at Oregon City, on the first Mondays in June and September annually.

The Criminal Court will hold its regular sessions on the second Mondays in June and September, at Oregon City.

COUNTY COURTS.

In the county of Tuality, last Mondays in April and July.

Champoeg, second Mondays in May and August.

Clatsop, second Mondays in April and July.

Yam Hill, first Mondays in May and Aug.

Clackamas, third Mondays in May and August.

Vancouver, third Mondays in April and July.

Lewis, last Mondays in May and August.

Polk, second Mondays in May and August.

The Presiding Judges of the County Courts are Judges of Probate, and Probate Courts are held monthly, and the day of holding the court appointed by the judge.

Blacksmithing.

NELSON & McDONALD,

HAVING rented Mr. H. Burns' old stand in Multnomah City, on the west side of the Willamette river, are now ready to supply their friends and customers with all kinds of manufactured iron and steel. They have a large stock of assorted iron and steel on hand, which will enable them to supply all orders in their line with despatch. They have now on hand a number of Diamond Cary Plows of the best quality, axes, drawing knives, mortising chisels, and edge tools of all kinds, warranted to carry a good edge, or no charge. All of which will be sold at a moderate price for good pay.

☞ Customers coming from the east side of the Willamette river to our shop for iron work, will be ferried free of charge. Feb. 19, 1846–1tf

Hat Manufactory,

Oregon City:

JOHN TRAVERS & WM. GLASER,

HAVING associated themselves together in manufacturing Hats at Oregon City, are now ready to supply their friends and customers with hats manufactured in Oregon. Although the profits are small, they confidently hope, by their prompt attention to business, to be able to furnish hats to the Oregon citizens at reduced prices.

Wool, beaver, otter, raccoon, wildcat, muskrat, mink, prairie wolf, and fox skins will be taken in exchange for hats. February 5, 1846–1tf

CITY HOTEL,

BY H. M. KNIGHTON,

Oregon City.

The traveling community are respectfully invited to call. The City Hotel is undergoing repairs, and the proprietor feels safe in saying that when completed, his customers will feel more comfortable, as every necessary attention will be rendered to make them so. His table shall not be surpassed in the territory. Those who favor him with a call from the west side of the river, will receive horse ferriage free. Jan. 30, 1846–1tf

The Red House & Portland.

JUST received, per Toulon of New York, on consignment, the following goods, viz:

20 cases wooden clocks ; 20 bbls. dried apples;
3 small mills; 1 doz. cross cut saws;
Mill saws and saw setts ; mill cranks, plough shares and pitch forks;
1 winnowing machine ; 100 casks cut nails;
50 boxes sadlers' tacks; 6 boxes carpenters' tools;
12 dox. hand axes; 30 boxes manufac'd tobacco;
50,000 cigars; 50 kegs white lead;
100 kegs paints ; 1-2 doz. medicine chests;
50 bags Rio coffee; 25 bags pepper;
200 boxes soap ;
50 cases boots and shoes; 5 do. slippers;
50 doz. cane seat chairs; 40 doz. wooden seat do.
50 doz. sarsaparilla; 10 bales sheetings;
4 cases assorted prints;
1 bale damask Tartan shawls;
5 pieces striped jeans ; 6 doz. satinett jackets ;
12 doz. linen duck pants ; 10 doz. cotton do. do.
12 doz. red flannel shirts;
200 doz. cotton hdk'fs; 6 cases white cot. flannels;
6 bales extra heavy indigo blue cotton;
2 cases negro prints ; 1 case black velveteen;
4 bales Mackanaw blankets ;
150 casks and bbls. molasses ;
450 bags sugar, &c., &c., for sale at reduced prices for cash, by

F. W. PETTYGROVE,

At the Red House, Oregon City, and at Portland, 12 miles below this city. Jan. 29, 1846–2w1

Willamette River at Oregon City

▷Wm. G. T'Vault, Editor of the *Oregon Spectator*, editorialized about the Willamette River in his Vol. I No. 2 issue of Feb. 19, 1846. For use here, the editorial is excerpted:

It will probably be interesting to many, and particularly so to those who anticipate visiting Oregon ... to know something of the Willamette, the Great Falls of which are now so rapidly coming into notice ... the most important water privilege west of the Rocky mountains.

[The river] traverses the whole length [of the valley] through a rich and fertile country and in many places, we might say, bounded with beautiful and luxuriant meadows, encircled with the lofty fir and interspersed with beautiful groves of oak.

But to describe the Willamette in its descent time and space will not permit minute description [but] on arriving at the Falls, the river spreads out into a wide, deep basin, and runs slowly and smoothly until within a half a mile of the Falls when its velocity increases, its width diminishes, eddies are formed in which the water turns back as if loathe to make the plunge but is forced forward by the water in the rear, and when still nearer, it breaks upon the volcanic rocks scattered across the channel and then, as if resigned to its fate, smoothes its agitated surges and [drops] down an almost perpendicular of twenty-five feet* presenting a somewhat whitened column. The rising mist, on a pleasant day, forms, in the rays of the sun, a beautiful bow—the whole forming a sight, the grandeur of which has to be seen to be appreciated.

*Editor T'Vault apparently "eye-balled" the drop of the fall. The U. S. Army Corps of Engineers measures the distance between the top and lower levels of the river at forty feet.

Plows! Plows! Plows!

$10,000 Reward for every one to attend to his own business.

THE subscriber begs leave to inform the public at large, that he has established himself in the Blacksmithing in general, in Oregon City, where he will keep on hand an assortment of Plows, which cannot be surpassed in the States. Persons wishing to purchase plows, can be accommodated with them, finished or unfinished. Also, Patent Pitch Forks, Hoes, Axes, and all kinds of mechanics' tools. As the subscriber has had long experience in machinery, he feels himself competent to execute all kinds of mill work, shingle machines, and thrashing machines of the best approved patents.

Gentlemen wishing to purchase any of the above articles, will do well to call and examine for themselves on Main street, Oregon City.

D. C. INGLES.

February 19, 1846–2tf

Eastward Bound.— Hugh Burns, Esq., informs us that himself and party will leave early in March next for the United States. Their route will be across the Rocky Mountains by way of the South Pass. Persons wishing to send east by the party, would do well to avail themselves of this opportunity. *Spectator. Feb 19, 1846*

▷We gave notice in our last publication that the postmaster general has contracted with H. Burns, Esq., to carry mail, for one trip only, from this place to Weston, Missouri—that letters mailed at any of the offices, post paid, would be forwarded. Postage only fifty cents on single sheets. We understand the construction given by some is, that Mr. Burns receives the fifty cents for his pay for carrying mail. This is a mistake. The postmaster general, we hope, will make better contracts that for the department. The terms of the contract are: Mr. B. receives 25 percent on the amount of postage that the department receives for sending letters east, and only fifty cents can be charged for a single sheet.

Spectator. Feb. 19, 1846

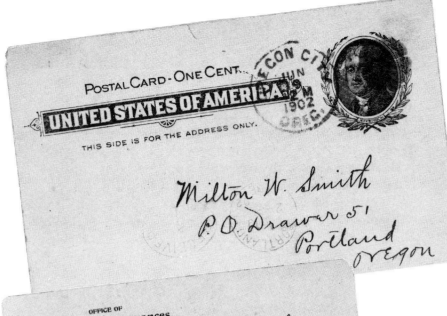

POSTAL CARD - ONE CENT
UNITED STATES OF AMERICA
THIS SIDE IS FOR THE ADDRESS ONLY.

Milton W. Smith
P. O. Drawer 51
Portland
Oregon

OFFICE OF
Recorder of Conveyances,
CLACKAMAS COUNTY

Oregon City, Ore., *June 20th 190 v*

Dear Sir: Your letter containing *Release of Mtg*
received. Please remit $ *75/* *,oo* _____ recording fees.
Under the salary law no papers can be filed until the
fees are paid.

Tom P. Randall
Recorder.

Chapter 5
Early Oregon Post Offices
Where's My Mail?

There had been postal service in the American colonies almost from the first, and little by little it was gradually expanded and improved. Benjamin Franklin was the Postmaster-general under British control but was removed at the time of the revolution—then reappointed by the Continental Congress. The movement of mail by the government was a challenge of the first degree because of competition by independent carriers, express companies and the high rates charged. Many of the private carriers issued adhesive stamps while the U. S. Post Office Department was still having postmasters write, in ink, "postage paid" – sometimes how much was paid – on covers (envelopes).

Pioneers were well on their way to Oregon before the Postal Reform Act of 1845 would help them with their letters. Even with the new regulations, there would be no U. S. post offices in Oregon to take advantage of the service until March of 1847.

Consider the 2,000 emigrants arriving as part of the Great Migration of 1843 and their desire for postal service. Mail to or from Oregon at that time was either carried back and forth by emigrants, or had to be left at Fort Vancouver with the Hudson's Bay Company with the hope that a ship captain would pick it up. It was not unusual for a letter sent east from the Oregon Country to require a wait of two years before the sender had a reply.

The Oregon Provisional government created the "Post Office Law" on December 23, 1845. Some of the pertinences were:

AN ACT to create and establish a Post Office Department.
1. *Be it enacted by the House of Representatives of Oregon Territory, as follows:* That there shall be established at **Oregon City** a general post office under the direction of a postmaster general who shall be elected by the House of Representatives... 2. The postmaster general shall establish post offices and appoint postmasters at all such places as shall appear to be expedient and provide for the carriage of mail to and from the same directing the route which route shall be considered a post road. ... 5. ...rates of postage for every letter conveyed in Oregon ... single sheet of paper not exceeding thirty miles, 15 cents; over thirty and not exceeding eighty miles 25 [cents]; eighty miles and not exceeding two hundred [miles] 30 [cents] two hundred miles 50 [cents]....

William G. T'Vault, the editor of the *Oregon Spectator*, was named Oregon's Postmaster General. As editor, he advertised for horsemen to carry the mail but because there were no post offices, no postage stamps, no roads and little mail due to the high rates, the plan was abandoned in a year.

It was also in 1847 that the first American adhesive postage stamps appeared in an effort for uniformity of rates.

Emigrants heading into the Oregon Country and to the California gold fields after mid-March 1850, had one last chance for getting mail from home. By then, the post office at Fort Laramie,

Wyoming (then in Nebraska Territory), opened.

With the growth of railroads, mail service improved but that did not help the far west until after 1869. In the meantime, contracts were let to stage coach operators as well as to individual carriers and to private express companies to carry mail beyond the western terminals. (And of course, much mail from the east coast was carried to San Francisco in ships.) For many years, even after the post offices were opened, the private carriers gave better service in the far west.

While all of this was very nice for those who had access to the service, as we have seen it was not yet for Oregonians as there were no United States Post Offices in Oregon until early 1847.

The first federal government post office west of the Rocky Mountains was at Astoria, Oregon which opened on the 9th of March 1847. Just twenty days later, March 29th, the post office at Oregon City opened. By the first of 1850 there were only four post offices in Oregon. Even though the order for offices in Portland and Salem was effective in the fall of 1849, the late Ed. Payne, a premier postal historian in Oregon, declared:

It is unlikely either Portland or Salem opened for business until spring 1850. Little mail was received in the last half of 1849 as all mail ships were held in San Francisco [because] the crews had left the ships for the gold fields. ... The dates of the [establishing] orders are not the actual dates the post offices opened for business.

Prior to 1855, letters were usually mailed "collect" with the amount of postage due written or hand-stamped on the upper *left* corner of the envelope.

Towns near Oregon City and Authorized Dates:	
(Arranged By Date)	
Portland	Nov. 8, 1849
Salem	Nov. 8, 1849
Milwaukie	Feb 1, 1850
Champoeg	Apr. 0, 1050 (intermittent service—closed Aug. 31, 1905)
Gladstone	June 30, 1890
West Linn	May 6, 1914
Canemah	(never had a post office)

The coming of mail was a great event for it heralded the start of a service that the so-called ordinary person could use. Until July 1, 1845, postage was expensive and express companies continued to handle much of the business mail. On that date a uni-

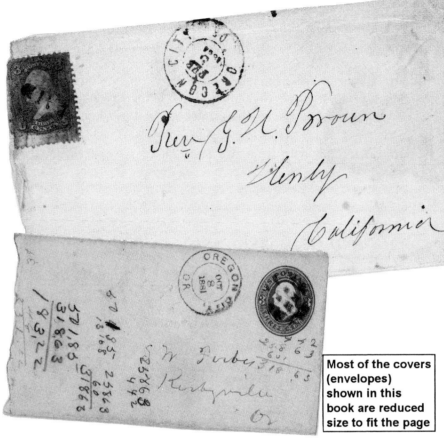

Most of the covers (envelopes) shown in this book are reduced size to fit the page

Placing the postage stamp on the top-left corner was a habit from pre-stamp days when postmasters hand-wrote the amout of postage there. Later, when automatic postmarking came along, the position was changed to the top right corner where it remains to the present time.

form schedule of postage was set up which cut the cost of a letter to only 10 cents per ½ ounce if the distance was over 300 miles. The rate between post offices anywhere within 300 miles, was 5 cents per ½ ounce. Eventually, nationwide letter postage was just 2 cents. (There were several changes in rates in the early days not included here.)

Payne reported:

As stamps were not sold in Oregon until 1852, 40 cent [the rate at that time], stamped letters from Oregon are unknown [to collectors]. The earliest *hand stamped* postal marking [for] Oregon City [was] March 1, 1850.

In the early days, for reasons unknown, folks tended to tear off left ends of covers to extract the letter. By the turn of the century, paper-knifes became common thus most envelopes have, since then, been opened at the top.

These were the days before typewriters so even business letters were handwritten. To get the best advantage of the postage, very thin paper was used as well as thin envelopes. These papers came in what was called 4-pound and 9-pound paper weight —"onion skin." (By contrast, the paper in this book is 70-pound.)

Example of 1898 cover that had been opened with a paper knife.

Postmasters had regulations to follow to make certain the mails moved smoothly and they were required to do official "paper-work" properly and on time. With the advent of Registered Mail and Postal Money Orders, rules became even more stringent. Every post office, regardless of its size, offered all of the services and nearly all post offices were open six days a week.

As in every business, there are customers who complain. With the post office it was usually "Where is my mail"? There were also many requests for improved service in the carrying of the mails. Sometimes hassles between patrons and postmasters became so serious that Postal Inspectors (earlier called "Special Agents") became involved.

An example of Special Agent involvement occurred at Oregon City and appears in the official records. The Special Agent, Quincy A. Brooks at Portland, received a complaint and followed up on it:

(File letter 222)   Portland, Oregon
                                                     July 23d, 1867

Postmaster
Oregon City Oregon

Sir:
        Deliver to D. M. McKinney Esq. the drop letter in your office addressed to him on payment of postage.

                        Yours etc.
                        Quincy A. Brooks
                        Special Agent

(File letter 223)   Portland, Oregon
                                                       July 23, 1867

Ed. Kelly Esq.
Postmaster
Oregon City, Oregon

Sir:
    D. M. McKinney Esq. of Oregon City complained that you refuse to deliver to him a drop letter in your office addressed to him, he is offering to pay postage due on it. I gave him an order on you for the letter, and trust that you will deliver it to him at once.
    Please inform me whether his complaint is correct, and if so, upon what ground you refused to deliver the letter.

                    Very respectfully
                    your obt. servant
                    Quincy A. Brooks
                    Special Agent

The available records do not include the nature of Mr. McKinney's complaint or in what manner Oregon City Postmaster Ed. Kelley responded. But there were apparently other violations of the rules at Oregon City for we find additional official mail:

(File letter 232)   Portland, Oregon
                                                       Nov. 8, 1867

R. F. Perkins, Esq.
San Francisco, Cal.

Friend Perkins:
    I have yours of the 18th ultimo in reference to the failure of the P.M. at Oregon City to forward weekly statements of his Money Order Business.
    Immediately upon the receipt of your favor of the 15th August in regard to the same subject, I made a visit to Oregon City, called on the P.M. and after explaining business, proceeded to read the "Riot Act." He made ample apologies, promised faithfully to "forsake the error of his ways" and to hereafter pursue the straight and narrow trail which leads to a better and more happy future.
    The bright hopes inspired by those fair promises however, have all been dispelled by your letter before me, which affords "confirmation strong proof from holy writ" that the "cuss" never intended to keep his word. I shall "go after" him again to-morrow, but entertain a lively impression that the best way to cure the obvious "sins of omission and commission" charged against that office is to secure the appointment of a new P.M.
    You can rely upon me to do all in my power to remedy the evil you

mention. I will write you again in a few days.

Truly & respectfully
Your obt. servant
Quincy A. Brooks
Special Agent

(File letter 237)

Oregon City, Oregon
June 27, 1868

E. B. Kelly Esq.
Late Postmaster
Oregon City, Oregon

Sir:

When you were relieved as Postmaster at this city by John Fleming Esq., your successor, on the 29th of last month, you should have turned over to him all books, blanks etc. appertaining to the Money Order Business, taking his receipt for same.

You are hereby instructed and directed to deliver to him immediately upon receipt of this note all books, blanks and other property of the Post Office Department appertaining to the Money Order Business, together with any other property belonging to the Department which may yet remain in your possession.

Very respectfully
Your obt. servant
Quincy A. Brooks
Special Agent

(File letter 238)

Oregon City, Oregon
June 27, 1868

John Fleming Esq.
Postmaster
Oregon City, Oregon

Sir:

You are hereby [sic] instructed to demand and take into your possession without delay all books, blanks and other property of the Post Office Department appertaining to said Money Order Business, together with any other property belonging to the Department which may yet remain in his possession, you giving to Mr. Kelly proper receipts for same.

Very respectfully
Your obt. servant
Quincy A. Brooks
Special Agent

Patera, in his book about Brooks' work, points out that Special Agents were essential for establishing post offices, the hiring and firing of postmasters and the designation of post roads and mail routes. He wrote:

These were times of dramatic growth and change in the West, and the role of Quincy Brooks in making the vital mails move with greater 'certainty, security, and celerity' was an important one.

In the last 100 years, the United States Post Office Department, and later the U. S. Postal Service, has made constant expansion in service as well as volume of mail handled until today postal operations stagger the imagination. ❖

**Oregon Trail Commemorative Postage Stamp
Issued February 12, 1993
First Day of Sale Official Ceremonies at Salem, Oregon
First Day postmarks at Salem and 37 Post Offices along the
Oregon Trail
Including Oregon City**

Chapter 6
Ship Building at the Falls of the Willamette

With two great rivers, the Columbia and the Willamette, being the earliest and easiest means of transportation, it was natural that ship building would spring up. The villages of Oregon City and Canemah (kah-NEEM-uh), the former below the falls, the latter stretched along the east side of the river starting just over a quarter of a mile above the falls (just over one mile south of the Oregon City Municipal Elevator—see pages 102-103) became noted for ship building. Canemah built more boats than Oregon City (27 to 9) but for our purpose, being so close together, the table provided includes both.

Canemah became the home poret for ship captains who ran schedules between Canema and up-river towns. Several of these men built substantial homes on the bluff near the river.

The area was once an Indian village* that became a land claim of Absolem Hedges in 1847. Hedges decided to make the most of the harbor-appearing river front so he set up a lodging house then started a ship building enterprise.

Ships were built facing north on pilings along the river's edge. When launching time came, ropes and blocks were released and the new ships entered the river sideways. The location of the shipyards was identified by Howard Klemsen, lifelong resident of Canemah, as being between Jerome and Paquet Streets, the latter now vacated near the south end of the community. Canemah is only about five city blocks long. Today the Southern Pacific railroad track is at the river's edge, the rails having invaded the area pushing south from Portland in 1869. About the only traces of the ship building industry seen today are some old pilings along the edge of the river.

Ship building was good for Canemah. Of the 36 ships listed in the Table, 27 were constructed at Canemah. The work kept

---

*The fact that an Indian village had been on the site was validated by young boys in the 1920's when they searched the river's edge looking for arrow heads. Howard Klemsen told the authors he "found plenty."

shipwrights busy making one or two vessels a year until a jump in 1857 saw four new ships built. There was a lull during the Civil War with no construction in 1862 or 1864 with only one river boat having been built in 1863. In 1865 there were four launchings. Between that year and the end of the era, 1878, only four more ships were built. A plausible reason for few ships built between 1861 and 1864 might also be attributed to the flood late in 1860. After rebuilding the facilities, what could be called a "one shot" surge in construction occurred in 1865 after which the industry petered out.

Apparently Hedges, and other builders at Canemah, sold every ship they built and there are yarns about nearly every one of them.

Did these boats make any money for their owners on the Willamette or did the ship owners pay big money to have them

Riverboats *Shoofly* (built 1870), and *ALICE* (built 1871), shown in Oregon City's boat basin. Both were built at Canemah. The curved railroad in foreground was for shuttling freight around the falls before the locks opened in 1873. Picture made in 1867.

The *Multnomah,* arrives at the 4th Street wharf in
Oregon City. The year was 1885.

SHIPS BUILT, OREGON CITY – CANEMAH
1851—1878
(36 Ships)

Ship Name	Paddle Driven	Where Built	Year	Tons	Length
		C= Canemah OC= Oregon City			
Active	stern	C	1865	498	148
Albany	stern	C	1868	382	127
Alice	stern	C	1871	457	150
Belle of Oregon City	side	OC	1853	54	96
*Canemah	stern	C	1851	88	135
Carrie Ladd	stern	OC	1858	—	126
***Carrie Norton	stern	C	1878	13	—
**Champion	stern	OC	1875	634	157
Dayton	stern	C	1868	202	117
Echo	stern	C	1865	273	122
Elk	stern	C	1857	60	—
Enterprise	stern	C	1855	—	115
Enterprise	stern	C	1863	194	120
Express	stern	OC	1854	69	111
Fannie Patton	stern	C	1865	297	132
Fanix x-Shoalwater	side	C	1852	49	93
Gazelle	side	C	1854	—	145
Hoosier No. 2	side	C	1855	—	—
Hoosier No. 3	side	C	1857	27	—
James Clinton	stern	C	1856	—	90
McMinnville	stern	C	1877	417	132
*Multnomah	side	OC	1851	—	108
Onward	stern	C	1858	120	125
Reliance	stern	C	1865	316	143
Relief	stern	OC	1858	229	118
Rival	stern	OC	1860	211	111
Sarah Hoyt	side	OC	1855	—	145
Senorita x-Gazelle	Side	OC	1855	—	145
Shoalwater	side	C	1852	—	93
Shoo Fly	stern	C	1870	317	126
Success	stern	C	1868	344	132
Surprise	stern	C	1857	120	130
Union	stern	C	1861	112	96
Wallamet	side	C	1853	272	150
*Yamhill	stern	C	1851	—	—
Yamhill	stern	C	1860	72	76

*Earliest built ships—1851. (Month built not found)

**Largest ship built   ***Last ship built during era 1851-1878   Source: *Stern Wheelers Up the Columbia*

carefully lowered over the falls into "greener" (money!) waters? Take the case of the *Wallamet* built in 1853. This big ship of 272 tons was slow to answer her helm. This made steering it's 150-foot long length in the narrow "up-river" over gravel bars and around snags a real challenge. There was not enough business coming the ship's way for the boat to make expenses. *Wallamet's* huge cargo space could never be filled.

With the captain, George Jerome, on board, the ship was most carefully lowered over the edge of the raging falls by block and tackle. Now, no longer limited to small up-river ports, the *Wallamet* worked the Portland-Astoria business then took a cargo to San Francisco. The *Wallamet* spent most of her days hauling freight on the Sacramento River.

In 1854 Canemah was the scene of a great tragedy when the *Gazelle*, Captain Robert Hereford, exploded at the dock. This was a new ship having made its maiden voyage on March 18. Around 6:30 on the morning of 8th of April, the ship had crossed the river from its home port, a little south of the village of Linn on the west bank, and tied up to the wharf at Canemah. The stop was intended to be brief. To be ready for departure, Engineer Moses Tonie, it was later established, had tied down the safety relief valve and had a full head of steam waiting for the order to head up river.

After just ten minutes at the dock, of the 60 persons on board 20 were killed. All remaining were injured (of whom four later died) when the ship blew up. Some of those killed were Judge Samuel L. Burch from Polk County, Rev. J. P. Miller from Albany O.T. and the ship's pilot John Clemens. Also killed was pilot J. M. Pudge of the *Wallamet* which was tied alongside. He, and several others on the second ship, were struck by flying wreckage. Most of the injuries were from scalding.

The steam engineer of the *Gazelle*, apparently realizing the boilers were about to blow, raced off the ship and out of sight and was not injured. The ship sank at the dock. A coroner's jury determined the explosion "resulted from the gross ... negligence" of the steam engineer for failure to keep sufficient water in the boilers and for "carrying more steam than was safe." The *Oregon Spectator* and the *Oregonian* carried detailed stories. The list of casualties and additional information appears in the Appendix.

In 1860 and again in 1890, the Willamette River flooded and caused much damage to riverside towns and villages. (Other severe flooding happened in 1935 and 1948.) At Canemah nearly all the buildings near the river were washed away. In Oregon City the flooded streets were occupied by men in row boats who had to watch out for floating logs.

During the 1860 flood, Captain George W. Taylor, held on and rode his ship, the *St. Claire,* over the swollen, crashing falls while dozens of folks on shore watched. His ship survived and he with it.

River boats were a major means of transportation therefore we see three in a single photograph. Foreground: *Success* (built in Canemah 1868) in boat basin. Center: *E.N. Cooke* (built in Portland in 1871). Background in locks: *Governor Grover* (built in Portland in 1873).

PEOPLE'S TRANSPORTATION CO.

The People's Transportation Co.'s Steamer **ALERT** will leave PORTLAND for OREGON CITY, Every Morning at 6½ o'clock, carrying the United States Mails. Returning—will leave for Portland at 1 P. M.

The Steamer **SENATOR** will leave OREGON CITY daily, (Sundays excepted) at 7 o'clock, A. M. Returning—will leave Portland at 2 o'clock, P. M.

The Steamer **RELIANCE** will leave CANEMAH every **Monday** and **Thursday** morning upon the arrival of the ALERT from Portland, for CORVALLIS and intermediate points.

The Steamer **FANNIE PATTON** will leave CANEMAH every **Thursday** and **Friday** for CORVALLIS and intermediate points.

The Steamers **ALBANY, SHOO FLY, ACTIVE** and **ECHO** will leave CANEMAH **ONCE A WEEK** for EUGENE CITY.

The Steamer **DAYTON** to DAYTON and McMINNVILLE Every **Monday, Wednesday** and **Friday.**

A. A. McCULLY,
President.

T. McF. PATTON, Sec'y,

Portland & Oregon City.

The favorite Stern Wheel Steamer

EXPRESS,

Jas. Strang, Master,

Leaves PORTLAND daily (Sundays excepted,) at 10 A.M., for OREGON CITY, and returning. leaves Oregon City daily, as above, at 4 P. M.

Portland, May 1st, 1858.   25tf

U. S. MAIL LINE.

OREGON CITY AND PORTLAND.

Daily Packet...**JENNIE CLARK**
Jos. Myrick,   Master.

THE JENNIE CLARK will run daily (Sundays excepted) in this trade, leaving

Oregon City......every day at 8 o'clock a. m.;
Returning, leaves

Portland.......................at 2 p. m.;
Touching at all intermediate points. For Freight or Passage apply on board.   [June 1855.

As the ship building business died and the railroads took the freight and passenger business, the importance of Canema declined. Some revival occurred when the trolley cars came through the village which is mentioned in Chapter 8.

In the mid-1980's, citizens of the area rose up in a bunch to protest when an old house was demolished to make room for an apartment. After considerable negotiation, much hassle and everyone finding themselves knee-deep in red-tape, Canemah was designated a National Historic District in October 1986 when the area was listed in the *National Register of Historic Places.* Today many of Canemah's majestic 19th century mansions have been restored. At few have interior conversions and have become a bed-and-breakfast and antique shops. ❖

The Capt. John Coburn House (1864) on the bluff in Canemah is Gothic Revival Style. The dwelling was restored and is presently a private home.

The Falls of the Willamette

"Awesome." "Magnificient."
Impediment to Commerce.
A quiet fight for control of its power.
The Great Fishing Hole of the River.

71

The Willamette Falls Locks of the U. S. Army Corps of Engineers.
The view is looking down-river through the Arch Bridge. The City
of West Linn is on the left and Oregon City is on the right.

72

Profile of the Willamette Falls Locks

Upper River South End | Guard Canal | Canal Basin | Lock No. 4 | Lock No. 3 | Lock No. 2 | Lock No. 1 | *Lower River North End*

Chapter 7
Willamette Falls Locks

Early shipping on the Willamette River was forced to stop at Oregon City because the 40-foot drop in the river at the falls frustrated shippers and prohibited transit until after a set of locks was built along the west shore.

The beautiful falls of the Willamette, where water tumbles over the edge of horseshoe-shaped, staggered-layers of basalt has been the subject of hundreds of thousands of photographs. And hundreds of thousands of fish have been caught below the falls many at the "hog-lines." (Hoglines are rows of fishing boats lashed side-by-side to each other, across the middle of the river, forming a seeming barrier of baited hooks through which one might think no up-stream bound fish could escape.)

Developing a region's resources is tied to transportation of goods and people and was immensely improved when the Willamette Falls Locks were opened to traffic.

By 1872, railroads had reached the Willamette Valley with lines carrying freight and passengers from Portland to as far as Roseburg. The freight rates were very high as there was no competition. Because shipping goods by water is traditionally lower cost, a means was needed to get goods over the waterfalls.

Before the locks were built, residents attempted to conquer the falls by portaging tons of cargo as well as passengers around it. At one period a short-line portage railroad operated for this purpose between Oregon City and Canemah, a mile upstream. Some ships were actually lifted, cargo and all, over the falls by "cordelling." This was accomplished by block and tackle attended by determined men with very strong muscles who pulled the ship up and over the falls into the river above.

73

OREGON CITY

Willamette Falls Locks

Willamette Falls

Portland I-205 Salem

The Willamette Falls Canal and Locks Company was incorporated in 1868 to overcome the limit on shipping imposed by the water fall. In 1870, the Oregon State Legislature approved $200,000 in state bonds to help pay for lock construction then issued a statement:

> The obstacles to the free navigation of the Willamette River at that place should be improved and freights carried on said river should be cheapened.

When the work was completed, ship captains found four locks, each with about 10-feet of lift as well as a canal basin and a guard lock at the south end of the project. The entire system is about 3,500 feet long.

Today's methods of construction require reinforced concrete but when the Willamette Locks were built its walls were of interlocked large and smaller square-cut stone.

The lock and canal company built the project but a private company, People's Transportation Company, opened the locks for business on New Years Day 1873. The cost for lockage was 50

Willamette Locks (left) and the famous horseshoe falls (right). This aerial view looks down-river. Oregon City is on the right.

The Willamette Falls Locks was entered in the *National Register of Historic Places* on February 5, 1974. One of the buildings in the complex, the Visitor's Center, was built in the early I900's and was used as a watch-site by the lock operators. This lock has the distinction of being the Corps of Engineers oldest multiple-lift lock. The project includes one of the oldest fish ladders in Oregon which was built and is operated by the Oregon Department of Fish and Wildlife.

Many boats with folks hoping to hook "the big one," are immediately down-river from the falls. The line of fishing boats lashed together is called a "hog line."

cents per ton of freight. The first year, about 25,000 tons passed through the locks. Passengers paid 10 cents each.

During the next 42 years there were several different owners. In 1915, the federal government bought the system from the Portland Railway, Light and Power Company for $375,000 and assigned the management and maintenance to the U. S. Army Corps of Engineers, Portland District. One of the first moves the Engineers made was to discontinue tolls.

Over the years, the Corps has improved this locked canal by modernization and better management methods. During a peak year in World War II, (1943), 2,246,211 tons of goods were locked around Willamette Falls. In the 1970's, the average annual tonnage was 800,000. In 1988, there were 5,619 separate lockages transporting 1,340,746 tons of cargo. This commerce continues to increase. Pleasure boats enjoy trips through the historic locks, which are open daily, with an average of 15 lockages every day.

The downstream entry to the locks is 26 miles from the confluence of the Willamette and Columbia Rivers. This convergence is 101 miles inland from the Pacific Ocean.

This system of locks is a fluid staircase between the upper and lower levels of the Willamette River. Each lock is 210 feet long and 40 feet wide. When a gate opens, it's only a matter of minutes for 850,000 gallons of water to flow by gravity into the next lower lock. Boats on the "downhill" trip take about half-an-hour to transit while ships moving upstream take a little longer, about 45 minutes.

Until 1940 the gates were operated by hand but now, modern, electrically-operated hydraulic pumps controlled by Lock masters in two closed-circuit television control stations with radios conduct lockage.

In the early days, dumping of all sorts of trash and garbage in rivers was common for rivers were considered by many to be waste conduits to the ocean. The Willamette, with huge paper mills dating back more than a century on each side—at Oregon City (east bank) and West Linn (west bank)—was no exception. Today however, millions of dollars are being spent on pollution control.

*   *   *

Visitors are welcome at the locks. In a picnic area there is a millstone on exhibit weighing about one ton that was retrieved from the river when the Corps was dredging in 1988. The stone is estimated at nearly a century old. A very large ship's anchor, of a design used in the 1800's, was also found and is displayed. ❖

While Visiting the Locks:

Visitors to the Locks can understand what's going on by observing these activities as ships and boats are being locked through the canal.

A major rule for everyone on boats is to wear a life jacket and shoes and stay seated. Because there is turbulent water near the entrances, small boats must wait for the green light before proceeding toward the locks then do not exceed 5 miles per hour. Never risk a life by swimming in the locks. The boat's pilot keeps a sharp eye on the lock operator for instructions. When the operator hands a safety line, the pilot holds on to it firmly and does not tie the rope to his vessel. Fenders should be on boats to prevent damage from bumping other craft or the sides of the canal. —Abridged from U.S. Army Corps of Engineers general guide.

The Main Line of what was called the "East Side Line" of the Oregon & California Railroad (now Southern Pacific) came though Oregon City. The 1-car train is a "payroll" train.

Chapter 8
Railroading and Trolley Cars

The railroad, which started laying track in Portland in 1868, finally crossed on a new bridge over the Clackamas River then ran through Oregon City and Canemah in 1869 on its way south. This marked the beginning of the end for the need for ships as the railroads captured most of the passengers as well as the fancy of shippers because it was new and exciting. But the freight rates were high which brought about the construction of the locks at the falls. With the locks in place on January 1, 1873, river shipping was now unimpeded by the falls between Portland and as far as Corvallis.

Even with this reprieve for shipping by boat, eventually trucks replaced the ships and in time trucks made severe inroads on the railroad's business as well.

Inter-city passengers now relied on the steam railroad rather than the river boats because service was faster. But soon a far more convenient means of commute with more frequent and even faster service came along in the form of electric trolley cars.

With the ships, one had to go to a specified pier on the river. With the trains, the passenger had to travel by whatever means to

Early trolley cars on this line bore women's names. The "Helen" was the first street car arriving in Oregon City from Portland and is shown at 6th and Main Streets in 1893. The top four crossarms on the line of poles along the left side of the street carry telephone lines—miles and miles of open copper wire. The lower shorter bottom crossarm, well separated from the telephone wires, carried A.C. power. The photograph does not clearly show the trolley wire but several of its supporting poles can be seen on the right side of the street. Although this was the main street of the city, it was not paved.

The Electric Hotel occupied the Chapman Block on west side of Main Street between 4th and 5th Streets. This is how it looked in 1892. Men in photo seem eager to go somewhere but it would be another year before the trolley car would make a stop here.

the depot. The trolley cars ran on Portland city streets and stopped at nearly every corner. In Oregon City, these interurban electrics whirred their way right through the middle of town. Once the demand was established, schedules were posted showing the electric cars moving between terminals every hour.

Ships and stream trains could not compete with the trolley cars. But even the interurban-electrics met their demise with the popularity of the automobile. Thus, little at a time the street cars were also forced out of business just as had been river boats and passenger trains.*❖

---

*Electric street railway buffs can see and ride on streetcars at the Oregon Electric Railway Historical Society's Trolley Museum and Park at Glenwood. This is on Highway 6 northwest of Forest Grove. The Park is open during summer months.

Trolley car "Kate" has just gone around "Bona, on a passing track while "Bona" waited then proceeded in the opposite direction. The interurban line from Portland was a single track with several "passing lanes." (lower) The Frank Busch Furniture Store in 1900 at 8th and Main Streets. It was a popular corner — the street car to Portland stopped here.

81

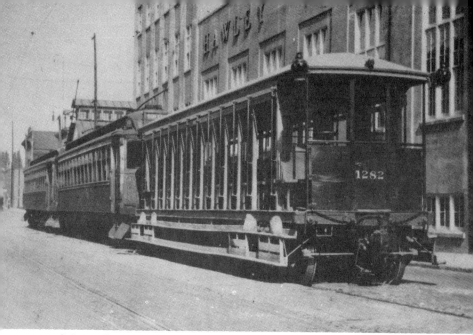

A 3-car Portland and Oregon City interurban in 1917 at 2nd and Main Streets, Oregon City. The open-air trailer was a summer-use car. In case of rain, the car was dropped at the "car barn" and exchanged for a closed car if passenger load demanded. Interurbans operated as "railroads" and were obligated to carry red-colored oil-burning tail lights. (lower) 2-car train ready to leave for Portland in 1911. Motorman was Mr. Fernandez. Other men are conductors, one for each car. Another car, in rear, awaits its scheduled departure.

Train at 9th and Main with 4th-of-July parade of decorated cars passing in 1931. (lower) Corner of 14th and Main Streets. Note car tracks in graveled street. Fretag's grocery store.

Digging up south end of Main Street in preparation for laying interurban track for the extension to Canemah in 1901. John McLoughlin's house is the white-front building on right side of street. The Canemah extension had to cross the Southern Pacific track but the project had been delayed due to obstinance of S.P. that didn't want to loose business to the electric "juice" powered cars. On a Sunday, the street car company moved in a track crew and installed crossing frogs on the S.P. rails with S.P. powerless to stop the work as no restraining order could be obtained because the court was closed.

Canemah Park

Howard Klemsen remembered his youth in Canemah when the open-air interurban electric trains went through Oregon City and Canemah to Canemah Park south of town. At the park, people left the cars at the base of the zigzag steps up the side of the riverside bluff to the park where there was a big dance floor protected from rain by a roof. He recalls many parties and picnics at Canemah Park.

The electric lines sponsored Sunday trains on "outings" over their systems to amusement parks, chataquas and picnic areas as a means of keeping passengers on the cars on weekends when business would otherwise be low.

Chapter 9
Oregon's Mint

The Provisional Government passed an Act on February 16, 1849 that provided for minting gold coins because coins of the United States were in short supply. Oregon City, with a population at that time of about 1,000, was designated the site for the mint. At the time the legislation for the mint passed, Oregon had been brought in to the United States as a Territory by the Congress. On March 2, the new governor arrived and immediately declared the coinage act unconstitutional as the federal government limited the right of coinage to itself.

But this "official business" did nothing to relieve the acute shortage of money-in-hand in Oregon so a committee of prominent citizens formed the Oregon Exchange Company to mint gold coins.

An engraver, Hamilton Campbell, made dies for a $5 gold coin. A blacksmith, Thomas Powell, built a press. The first coins were probably struck in March 1849.* These coins were called "beaver" coins because they have an engraving of a beaver on one side.

A few months later a $10 gold piece was designed and also struck at Oregon City. The engraving was by Victor Wallace. These coins were heavier by about eight percent than was needed so most were bought up for melting. Beaver Coins of Oregon are rare today.

---

*Some writers claim the Oregon City mint was the first mint on the west coast but private coinage also started in San Francisco that year. The exact startup dates for both mints do not appear in contemporary coin encyclopedias. NOTE : During the financial pinch of 1907, Oregon was plagued by another shortage of coins that was temporarily relieved when two men at Baker City produced coins in November of that year. These coins did not bear the legend "In God We Trust" instead read "In Gold we Trust." For picture and more information see *Flagstaff Hill on the National Historic Oregon Trail, Baker City, Oregon.*

Chapter 10
Images

Our "Images" are historical views. In the photograph on this page is a scene from the bridge of the 1890 flood that indundated river-side towns including Oregon City.

On the facing page, the flat-land at the far end of the railroad tressle (top) is the area at the end of the 2,000 mile long Oregon Trail. As 1890 flood picture shows (lower), this land was under water.This is the area where a new End of the Oregon Trail Interpretative Center will be built in the mid-1990's.

Clackamas County Courthouse (top) in Oregon City in 1886 overlooking the Willamette River. One of several livery stables (lower) in Oregon City in 1885. (Opposite page at top) The Courthouse in 1889. Scene from across the river, The Courthouse and the river boat *Altona* in 1888.

89

Oregon City in 1874

New Ford Model T cars being off-loaded from Southern Pacific freight cars at 14th and Main Streets, Oregon City. These new cars were consigned to The Pacific Highway Garage. The year was 1915. The touring car with top in place at right does not appear to be a Ford. As there is a catenary (overhead power line for street cars) in the view, it appears these freights arrived between runs of the trolley cars. For some time, Oregon City had an Ordnance against the electric line's hauling freight cars on city streets.

Oregon City Telephone Office in 1918 was located at 514 Main Street. The 6-position Attendance Cabinet (commonly called a switchboard) was battery operated and had hundreds of miniature lights, one for each "jack" that connects to a subscriber's line. (The ceiling lamp is oil.) Picture shows five operators and the Chief Operator. Four of the operators are not busy and are looking at the photographer. The Chief Operator handled calls referred by an operator including settling arguments. The white panels above each position is a "directory" of all the subscribers listed alphabetically. Most regular operators "knew the board" and what number was assigned to each customer. Patrons could ask an operator for another subscriber by name or phone number. This switchboard apparently has about 200 lines. Numbers started with No. 1 with the lowest often restricted to the telephone company's own needs. The "crank" on the corner of each board rang a phone after the operator made the connection. This "common battery" switchboard was noted for being trouble-free and remained unchanged, except for the addition of a dial and power ringer, until the late 1930's.

The Huntley Brothers owned and operated the Drug Store and the town's book and stationery store. These men were also telegraph operators or hired a "brass-pounder" for the book store was the Oregon City agency for *Postal Telegraph*, a competitor of Western Union. (lower) Ed Johnson owned the "O.K. Barber Shop" at 705 Main Street. He, as "boss," worked the chair farthest from the front door.

Oregon City's steps. Many folks could not go shopping or get home without negotiating steps. The 5th Street Steps in 1900 and (right page) the 7th Street Steps (1892). The 7th Street Steps were often blocked by trains that stopped for water. The railroad is still there but the water tank and steps are long gone.

94

The mills (left page) as seen from the west side of the river in 1892. Clearly seen here are the three levels of the town. Businesses (this page) along 7th Street at the Oregon City end of the bridge. Thousands of people line the river bank to watch a boat races during "Territorial Days" in 1936. Steamers are *Anna Commings* and *N. R. Lange.*

View looks northwest from the bluff shows 5th and Main Streets,
Willamette River and the Arch Bridge in 1936. 5th Street here is
Pacific Highway 99E that passes under railroad. The Arch Bridge
(lower) with "hog line" of fishing boats in mid-river.

A drayage firm has just off-loaded a huge vault for the Bank of Oregon City as dozens of kibitzers gawked. Probably a summer picture as McKittrick's Shoe Store window shade is down. The city's newspaper, the *Enterprise,* was on the corner. (lower) In 1896 bankers H. L. Kelly, Herman Jones, E. G. Caufield, Charles Caufield did not often sit down at their jobs. Not seen is probably at least one .44 caliber pistol strategically placed to be ready in case there was an "emergency."

Oregon City Public Library

The city had the first public library in Oregon with quarters moved among several buildings over the years. The present building is at the corner of 7th and John Adams Streets on the lot seen at top opposite page. There was so little traffic in 1900 the daisies grew wild in the street! The building had a face-lift and expansion about 1938. Story telling on the lawn of Library Park has always been popular and continues to the present time. Nearly all public libraries have extensive story telling activities aimed at orienting young minds to the fun and value of books at an early age.

"When One Is Finished With All the Gadgets Out There, Come Back to Good Old Books."
—Bert Webber MLS

...and daisies grew in the street.

Oregon City Public Library today

Chapter 11
Oregon City's
Vertical Street

Getting the city's first elevator built was a challenge for the people, for politicians and for contractors who wanted too much money. But the elevator was opened at last marking an end to having to hike the steps. The Municipal Elevator has always been a major attraction and continues so to the present time.

Oregon City, A Three-Level Town

When the area that makes up Oregon City was formed, it produced three tiers or levels of land. The town was built nearest the river on the first level. It was not long before there was expansion to the second level 100 feet above which in time saw need for more space on the third level—another 200 feet higher.

On the "ground floor" were the first stores, hotels, and homes. The wharves along the river front were there as was the railroad and later electric trolley cars as well as the manufacturing plants. Access to the second level was up very steep streets and by slippery (in rainy weather) wooden and later stone steps. In 1913 a municipal elevator was built to the second level for the convenience of the people. (The present elevator was built in 1954.) The third level reaches all the way to the mountains.

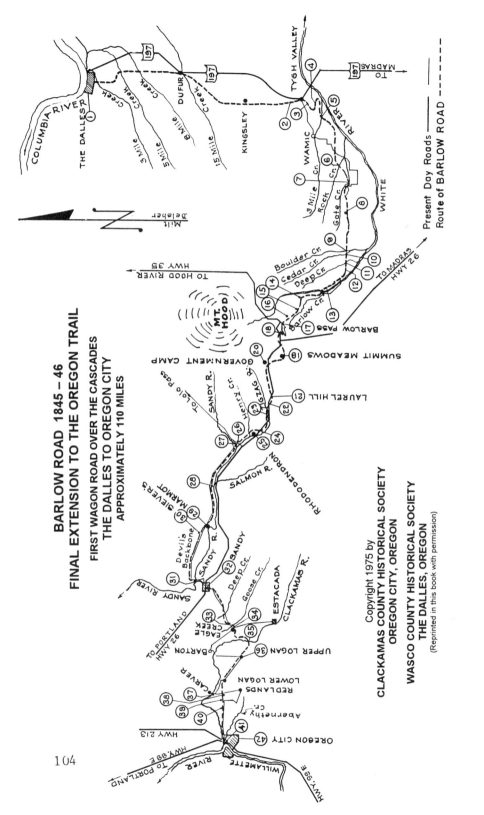

BARLOW ROAD 1845 – 46
FINAL EXTENSION TO THE OREGON TRAIL
FIRST WAGON ROAD OVER THE CASCADES
THE DALLES TO OREGON CITY
APPROXIMATELY 110 MILES

Present Day Roads
Route of BARLOW ROAD

Copyright 1975 by
CLACKAMAS COUNTY HISTORICAL SOCIETY
OREGON CITY, OREGON

WASCO COUNTY HISTORICAL SOCIETY
THE DALLES, OREGON
(Reprinted in this book with permission)

104

Historic Interest Sites
Sites in Hood River & Wasco Counties
(approx. 58 miles)

MAP
NUMBER

1   The Dalles
2   Tygh Ridge route into Tygh Valley
3   Tygh Valley Camp
4   Up steep hill to Wamic Plateau
5   3 Mile Creek crossing (Marker in Wamic)
6   Rock Creek crossing
7   Gate Creek crossing/No. 1 toll gate area
8   Immigrant Springs (sign)
9   Boulder Creek Crossing (name changed
       back from Crane Creek)
10 Cedar Creek Crossing (name changed
       back from Forest Creek)
11 Deep Creek Crossing (name changed
       back from Klip Creek) (marker)
12 White River (Little Laurel) Hill
13 Old White River Station (marker)
14 Klinger's Camp (marker)
15 Grindstone Camp (sign)
16 Devil's Half-Acre (marker)
17 Barlow Pass (marker)

Sites in Clackamas County
(Approx. 52 miles)

17 Barlow Pass (marker)
18 Unknown woman's grave (marker)
19 Summit Meadows/No. 3 toll gate
20 Government camp (marker)
21 Laurel Hill (marker)
22 Meeting Rock (recently demolished)
23 Brow Log (only crossing Zigzag River)
24 No. 5 toll gate (marker)
25 Rhododendron. Henrty Creek crossing
       (marker)
26 Site: Hudson's Bay Co. Trading Post
27 Sandy River first crossing (marker)
28 Site: Rock Corral camp
29 Marmot (Over Devil's Backbone
       7 miles)
30 Siever's Place
31 Francis Revenue's Place/No. 2 toll gate
       Sandy River second crossing (marker)
32 Sandy (marker)
33 Ruts down hill into Foster's Place
34 Philip Foster's Place
       Eagle Creek (marker)
35 Feldenheimer's Ford
       Clackamas River crossing
36 Upper Logan
37 Baker Cabin (marker) Indian Rock
38 Deep ruts
39 Holcomb School (ruts south side yard)
40 Holcomb Hill
41 Abernethy Creek (marker)
42 Oregon City – End of Oregon Trail
       (2,200 miles) (marker) 1845

OREGON CITY

Lower level — original town

OREGON CITY

WEST LINN

←Portland I-205 Salem→

Appendix B
The Willamette Meteorite

Oregon City has always been closely associated with the Willamette Meteorite for a number of reasons. A couple are:

1. The *Oregon City Enterprise* and the *Oregonian* ran stories about it. The fact that the articles mentioned Oregon City and one of the papers was an Oregon City newspaper brought publicity to Oregon City.

2. At one time a proposal was made that Oregon City be the permanent location for the meteorite's public exhibit—more publicity for Oregon City.

Although this very famous meteorite—the largest ever discovered in the United States—generated world-wide publicity for Oregon City, the fact is, it was not found in Oregon City or even on the east side of the Willamette River where Oregon City is situated. The meteorite was discovered in a desolate heavily forested area about two miles northwest of the village of Willamette. The settlement was on the west side of the river and today is a district within the City of West Linn.

The name "Willamette Meteorite" was given to this nobel meteorite by Henry A Ward, a scientist, in 1904. Ward called it "The most interesting meteorite, nobel in size and wonderful in physical features." Ward, an expert in meteorites had traveled across the United States to see and study the meteorite which had gained much newspaper notoriety since is was discovered by Ellis Hughes in the fall of 1902.

Hughes recalled years later:

I was coming home from work where I had been cutting wood for the Willamette School. I saw this big rock but didn't think anything about it. I'd never seen it before. The next day when I came from work I saw half a broken saw lying near the rock. It was very rusty. Evidently some woodsman had dropped it there. I sat down on the rock. It was about 1½ feet above the ground and very flat.

Bill Dale came by and said, Hughes, have you seen this rock before?"

108

Willamette meteorite shown upside-down to illustrate the cavernous depressions probably produced by sitting in damp earth for thousands of years. When discoverd, the rounded top, resembling a Volkswagen "bug," was showing through the surface of the ground. This is the largest meteorite yet discovered in the United States.

Yes, I said, I saw it yesterday. Then I picked up a large white stone and started to hammer on the rock. It rang like a bell.

"Hughes," Dale said to me, "I'll bet that is a meteorite."

It would probably be there yet but my wife had ideas. She was afraid somebody would go up and get it the next day.

Hughes expressed some worry that if word leaked out, curiosity seekers would come along and hack off pieces of it as souvenirs. The meteor had been found on land belonging to the Oregon Iron and Steel Company of Oswego. Hughes had bought his property from that firm, which was adjacent to it, so he determined to dig up the object and haul it to his property. All that fall and into the spring of 1903 he worked very quietly preparing to move the meteorite.

The shape of this meteorite has been described as "bell-like" or even like a Volkswagen "bug." Its weight was determined to be just over 31,000 pounds. When he found it, the meteor was upside down, that is, the top was underground and the nearly flat surface of the bottom was sticking out of the ground.

Because it was obviously much to heavy to haul away merely

The Willamette Meteorite—General Data

Weight: 31,107 pounds when readied for rail shipment
Dimensions: 10-feet 4-inches long
             7 feet wide
             4 feet 3 inches high (–Haas: *Table Rock Sentinel*)
Analysis: 91.5% iron
             8% nickel
             cobalt (trace); phosphorus (trace)
Specific gravity: 7.7   (–Lange: *The Willamette Meteorite*)

1) The Willamette meteorite is the largest "oriented" meteorite in the world in the form or a broad cone. 2) When first landed it probably weighed more than twenty tons but lost weight due to rusting. 3) The meteorite probably did not land where it was found but probably in Canada during the last ice age after which it rode down to Washington on the ice sheet, then floated into place on an iceberg during the great Missoula flood when the huge ice dams broke up.   (–Haas: *Table Rock Sentinel*)

On one side it offers the greatest known instance of aerial erosion, helped by fusion. No holes and furrows due to aerial attrition have been offered by any other meteorite whether of the iron or stone class.   (–Ward: *Proceedings of the Rochester Academy of Science*)

The great hollows and deep pits which characterize the surface of the mass combine with its enormous size to make this the most remarkable and interesting meteorite known.
                         (–Hovey: *Journal of the American Museum*)

The only larger meteorite in the United States is the Ahnighito (Cape York) meteorite which was discovered in Greenland in 1894 and moved to the United States by the U.S. Navy in 1897. It weighs is 36½ tons.   (–Ward: *the Willamette Meteorite*)

with a rope and a horse, Hughes used his ingenuity. With 10-foot long trunks of trees closely fitted and bound together to form a wagon bed, be made a cart. For wheels he cut rounds (trunks) of trees about 12-inches thick. For axles, front and rear, be again turned to logs. He kept the "wheels" in place with steel pins driven through the ends of the logs like cotter-keys. With his wife, a teen-age boy and his horse and a capstan, he pulled the meteorite from the earth and got it onto the cart. He had borrowed rope and pulleys from the paper mill on the nearby river. The move took about three months with progress limited to a few feet on some days, no motion at all at times, and a great triumph one day when the cart was moved 150 feet! And all the time nobody knew about

Ellis Hughes, who discovered the great Willamette Meteorite in 1902, is pictured in 1937. Although several courts found differently, he died in 1942 still of the opinion that he owned it.

this strange activity in the forest.

Once on his property, Hughes set up a shed over it and charged admission of 25 cents for the public to view it. Apparently one of the visiting viewers was an attorney for the Oregon Iron and Steel Company. The Company was supposed to have tried to buy it for as little as $50 then $100. But Hughes refused to sell. Then on November 27, 1903, the company sued for recovery claiming the meteor belonged to the Company and it had been sneaked off its property.

The newspaper story said:

> It has been reported on the streets and there are many who accept the rumor, that the meteor was actually discovered on land adjoining that of the parties who now have it in possession and claim sole title thereto. The report is to the effect that the specimen was clandestinely removed onto the land of those now having the meteor in possession before the discovery of the heavenly monster was announced.

As we have seen, that was true. The court decided in favor of the Iron Company and determined the meteorite had a value of $150.00. But that was not the end of it. Other suits followed with poor Ellis Hughes losing every one of them, including an appeal to the Oregon Supreme Court.

With the meteorite, now legally in the hands of the Oregon

Iron and Steel Company, the firm arranged to display its curiosity at the Lewis and Clark Exposition in Portland in 1905. But Oregon was about to lose its famous rock-o'-the-heavens.

After the exposition closed, Mrs. William A. Douglas II paid $20,600 for it and presented it to the American Museum of National History in New York where it still resides. When being readied for shipment, it was placed on a scale by the railroad and its weight determined to be 31,107 pounds.

In preparation for the centennial of the State of Oregon in 1959, then Oregon's Governor Robert D. Holmes wrote to the Museum of Natural History to seek the loan of the meteorite for exhibit in Oregon during the celebration. The museum responded favorably but noted that the loan would be impossible. This was because when the Hayden Planetarium had been built in 1936, it was build around the Willamette Meteorite and there was no door large enough through which the meteorite could pass.

*   *   *

Ellis Hughes lived out his life as a farmer but harbored resentment over the way his discovery had been handled in the courts. Although he died in December 1942 at age 83, he is remembered in scientific and judicial circles as the "finder and loser of the largest meteorite ever discovered in the United States. ❖

OREGON SPE

PRINTOR AND PRINTER] .... "THE AGITATION OF THOUGHT IS THE BEGINNING OF

APRIL 18 1854 ⸺ OREGON CITY, OREGON TERRITORY, FRII

AWFUL EXPLOSION
OF STEAMER GAZELLE !!
Twenty-eight Lives Lost !!!
THIRTY OTHERS WOUNDED!!

The Wallamette Falls Co.'s new steamer "Gazelle" left her wharf, last Saturday morning at 6 o'clock, and had landed at the upper landing at Canemah, when at about twenty minutes before seven, a terrible explosion of her boilers blew her into atoms, killing nearly thirty persons and wounding as many others.

Probably a more heart-rending scene has never occurred on the Pacific coast. As soon as the smoke cleared away a little, hundreds of citizens, who were very ready to assist the dying, gathered on the wreck, and the work of aid commenced.

Fragments of bodies were found scattered in every direction ; some were blown into the river, others on to the shore ; but the greater part of the killed found, were lying about the deck forward, among all kinds of fractured machinery and freight. A more horrible sight can hardly be imagined. Mr. David Page, Chief Supt. of the company,

Continued next column

had his head literally dashed to pieces and could not have been recognized by other means than his clothes. Many others were badly mutilated.

We have hurridly collected these particulars and give the names of those known (up to 10 p.m.) to be killed and wounded.

List of Killed
David Page, San Francisco, the Co.'s superintendent.
David Woodhall, Mich.
Rev. Mr. Miller, Albany
John Bloomer, (deck hand)
Joseph Hunt (surveyor) Michigan
Mr. Hatch. (deck hand)
John Daly, (cabin steward)
John Clemmens, (pilot)
David Fuller, Portland
Mr. Wadsworth, (passenger)
Judge Birch, (passenger), Luckmiuke, O.T.
James White, Salem
John K. Miller, (deck hand)
J. M. Fudge (pilot of *Wallamet*)
Mr. Morgan, Lacreole
A Spaniard (name unkn)

Missing
Mr. Hill, Albany, O.T.
Daniel Lowe (passenger)
Mr. Knaust (formerly of steamer *Whitcomb*
Daniel McLane, Lafayette, Ind.
Three firemen whose names have not been learned and two strangers are known to be gone in addition to above.

Wounded, Scalded, &c.
Capt. R. Hereford (of *Gazelle* scalded
Mr. Prevaut, (passenger) scalded
B.F. Newby, (passenger) badly scalded
Mrs. Miller, (lady of

Continued next page

Rev. Miller) had two ribs broken

Mate Boyd, both arms broken

Miss Pell, slightly scalded and a gash in the forehead

J. Herald, scalded

Jas. Partlow (pilot) slightly hurt

Michael M'Gee (deck hand) scalded

H. Royce, scalded

David Davis, sligfhtly hurt

Mr. Piant (2d engineer) scalded

Chas. gardiner, slightly scalded and arm broken

Crawford Dobbins, one leg gone—amputated

Preston S. Black (cabin steward) slightly scalded

Robt. Shortess, slightly wounded

Jas. Stanfield (steward) slightly wounded

Henry Traulk, badly scalded

Several others scalded and wounded whose names we have not.

Two brothers (Messers Latshaw); Moses Tonie, 1st engineer; Z. Crowell, clerk; and Mrs. Piant and child together with the little daugher of the Rev. Mr. Miller ecaped uninjured.

This distressing disaster has thrown a deep shade of gloom over the whole community. Stores, shops, iron-works, mills &c. are closed for the afternoon—and business is generally hushed. In Canemah a feeling of intense grief is manifested by nearly every one seen. Col. White, Mr. Post, Jno P. Brooks and others generally opened their places of business and spare rooms for the benefit of the wounded and for the dead bodies until they are recognized and cared for by the respective friends.

Artist's concept of the exploding *Gazelle* in April 1854. The boiler blast killed 28, injured 30. Ship's engineer was blamed.

The Webbers have presided at the Oregon Authors Table during the Oregon State Fair since the beginning of this book exhibit a decade ago. During the 12-day event, the fair enjoys about 800,000 patrons thus the fair has become a valuable test market for those Oregon authors who are invited to participate. Webber books are available through all independent book dealers nationwide.

About the Authors

Bert and Margie Webber have worked together to bring out new books about Oregon for several years. Bert is a Research Photo-journalist with degrees in Journalism and in Library Science. He has spent most of his life snooping for "good stuff" to photograph and to write about. Margie, with a degree in Nursing, finished a career as a Registered Professional Nurse then joined her husband in the preparation of new books. They have four grown children and at the moment seven lively grandchildren. They live in Oregon's Rogue River Valley.

Bibliography

Anderson, Martha. *Black Pioneers of the Northwest 1800-1918.* (private print) 1980.

Babcock, Chester D. and Clare A. *Our Pacific Northwest.* McGraw-Hill. 1963.

Bancroft, Hubert Howe. *History of Oregon.* Vol I and II. [Written by Francis Fuller Victor] Hist. Co. 1886.

Barlow Road. (Bicentennial Ed. 3rd Printing) Clackamas County Hist. Soc. & Wasco County Hist. Soc. 1976.

Boggs, Winthrop S. *Foundations of Philately.* VanNostrand. 1955.

Breen, Walter. *Complete Encyclopedia of U. S. and Colonial Coins.* Doubleday. 1979

Corning, Howard McKinley. *Willamette Landings.* Binford & Mort. 1947.

Dublin, Wm. Brooks. *Trail's End Oregon City Where the Past Meets the Present.* Green 1982.

Elliott, T. C. "The Origin of the Name Oregon," in *Oregon Historical Quarterly,* Vol XXII June 1921.

Evans, James A. and Bert Webber. *Flagstaff Hill on the National Historic Oregon Trail.* Webb Research Group. 1992.

Gardner, Wilmer. (Ed.) *Over One-Hundred Years of Old Oregon City.* Clackamas County Hist. Soc. 1976.

Haas, Gordon. "Catch A Falling Star" in *Table Rock Sentinel.* Vol. 11 No. 4. July/Aug. 1991 pp. 18-26.

Helbock, Richard W. *Oregon Post Offices 1847-1982.* LaPosta. 1982.

Hoffman, Charles S. and Bert Webber. *The Search For Oregon's Lost Blue Bucket Mine; The Stephen Meek Wagon Train of 1845.* Webb Research Group. 1992.

Hovey, Edmond O. "The Willamette Meteorite" in T*he American Museum Journal.* July 1906 pp. 105-116.

Johansen, Dorothy and Charles M. Gates. *Empire of the Columbia.* Harper & Row. 1957.

Landis, Robert L. *Post Offices of Oregon, Washington and Idaho.* Patrick. 1969.

Lange, Erwin F. *The Willamette Meteorite.* (private print) [1962].

McLoughlin, John. *John McLoughlin's Business Correspondence 1847-48* William R. Sampson, Ed. Univ. of Wash. Pr. 1973.

_____*Letters of Dr. John McLoughlin 1829-1832.* Burt Brown Barker, Ed. Binford & Mort. 1948.

Mills, Randall V. *Stern-Wheelers Up the Columbia.* Pacific Books. 1947.

Oregon End of the Trail. [American Guide Series]. Binford & Mort. 1951.

Patera, Alan H. *Your Obedient Servant; The Letters of Quincy A. Brooks, Special Agent of the Post Office Dept. 1865-1867.* Raven. 1986.

Palmer, Joel. *Journal of Travels Over the Rocky Mountains to the Mouth of the Columbia River Made During the Years of 1845 and 1846....* Cincinnati, 1847.

Payne, Edward R. *Oregon Post Offices and First Postmasters.* private print. [*ca* 1959].

_____. "Oregon Territorial Post Offices and Handstamped Postal Markings" in *Oreg. Hist Quarterly.* Vol. 60 No. 4. Dec. 1959 pp 475-488.

"Plaque Placed in Memory of Pioneer Steamer Victims" in *Oregon Sunday Journal.,* May 14, 1933.

Pruett, J. Hugh. "The Willamette Meteorite" in *Popular Astronomy.* March 1939 Vol. 47. pp. 148-150.

"To Persons Wishing To Send Letters East" in *Oregon Spectator.* Vol.1. No.1 Feb. 5, 1846.

Turnbull, George S. *History of Oregon Newspapers.* Binford & Mort. 1939.

Webber, Bert. *Wrecked Japanese Junks Adrift in the North Pacific Ocean.* YeGalleon. 1984.

Welsh, William D. *A Brief History of Oregon City and West Linn, Oregon.* private print. 1941.

Wiley, Nell and Vera Lynch. "Big Industry Comes to Willamette Falls" in *Clackamas County Historical 1964-1965* Clackamas County Hist. Soc. [1965].

"Willamette River [at Oregon City]" in *Oregon Spectator.* Vol. 1. No. 2. Feb. 19, 1846.

Winther, Oscar O. *The Great Northwest.* 2nd Ed. Knopf. 1964.

Yarnes, Thomas D. *A History of Oregon Methodism.* Ore. Methodist Conf Hist Soc. [1957].

Illustration Credits

Index

Illustrations are shown as **bold** *italic*

FIRE! —On Saturday the 7th instant, the plank kiln of Dr. John McLoughlin was discovered to be on fire, which was, however, soon extinguished by the united efforts of the Americans, British, Irish, Kanakas, (alias Sandwich Islanders) and Indians. On that occasion it was hard to tell which nation had the preference. It was a perfect heterogeneous mass on conglomerated guttural sounds, *"Hiack 'tsuch"* was the only audible sound we could hear and that was from the doctor himself, which means *"hurry! water!!* Loss sustained about 1,000 feet of lumber. Spectator Feb. 19, 1846